Fabulous Fruits

Recipes for every season

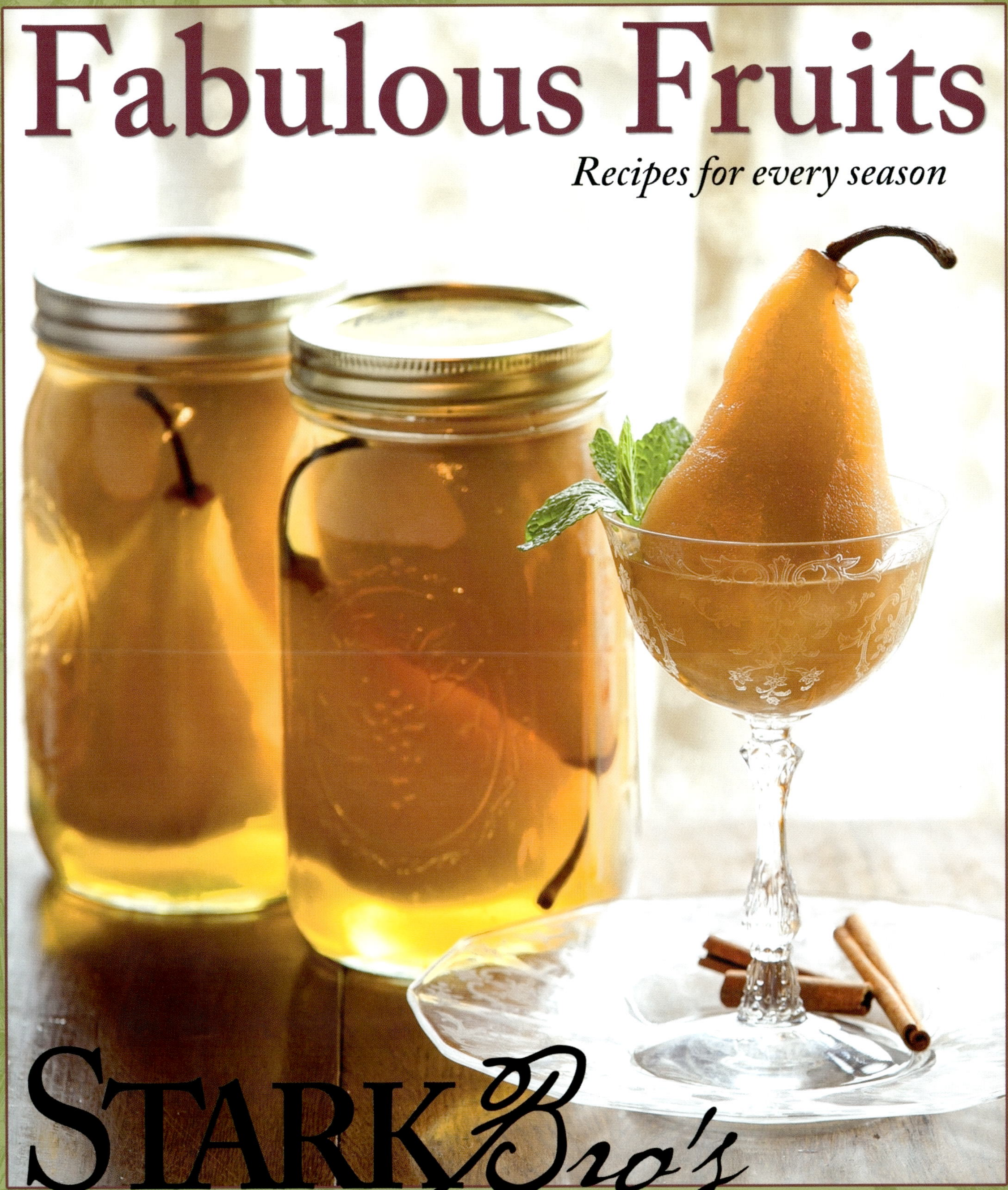

STARK Bro's

A GROWING LEGACY SINCE 1816

How to get maximum enjoyment from this book ...

- Always read a recipe through before you begin cooking. This will assist you in putting together your shopping list, will clarify the cooking steps and help to avoid mistakes midway through the process.
- When you are ready to cook, lay out all of the ingredients and measure them. This cuts preparation time and is a much more relaxed way to work.
- Using the correct utensils, pots and pans will give you a superior result, and will also make serving easier.
- Use your creativity to alter recipes to suit your own tastes. Remember, there are no new recipes, just adaptations of existing ones!
- When you organize your menu plan, select recipes that complement each other. Choose only one difficult recipe per menu, and look for easier recipes to accompany it. Accent the natural flavors of the simpler dishes to elevate them.
- Buy only the freshest ingredients, and those that are in season. Patronize your local farmers' market for the best produce, and don't forget your own back yard, where you might be growing your own fabulous fruits!
- This is your book, so don't be afraid to make notes next to the recipes you like and what adjustments you made.
- About abbreviations: *TBS.* is tablespoon; *tsp.* is teaspoon; *oz.* is ounce or ounces; *lb.* is pound.
- Relax, and enjoy your cooking and baking time. It's a form of art and expression, and a way to nourish your body and spirit. Let your creative nature come out!

Acclaim Press
— Your Next Great Book —
P.O. Box 238
Morley, MO 63767
(573) 472-9800
www.acclaimpress.com

Fabulous Fruits
Recipes for Every Season
Created to celebrate 200 years of Stark Brothers Nurseries & Orchards Co.

Author: Karen Mitcham-Stoeckley
Photography and Design: Curt Dennison

ISBN: 978-1-942613-20-6 / 1-942613-20-2
Library of Congress Control Number: 2015914303

First Printing: 2015
Printed in the United States of America
10 9 8 7 6 5 4 3 2 1

This publication was produced using available information.
The publisher regrets it cannot assume responsibility for errors or omissions.

Contents

Introduction to *Fabulous Fruits*

In October of 1816, a group of settlers from Kentucky crossed the Mississippi River at the spot that is now Louisiana, Missouri. The group's leader, James Hart Stark, brought a bundle of apple scions from his father's orchard so that he could start his own nursery. James had learned the art of grafting fruit trees as a young man, and knew that selecting and cultivating better fruit trees would make him a success. (Before his arrival, Missouri apple trees were randomly planted from seed, which rarely results in a tree like its parent.) People came from miles around for James' superior trees and fruit, and that was the beginning of Stark Bro's Nurseries & Orchards Co., the world's oldest continuously-operating nursery.

Stark Bro's is responsible for discovering the Red Delicious and Golden Delicious apples, as well as 300 varieties of other tree fruit, berries, nuts and ornamentals. Home orchardists choose Stark® trees and fruiting plants for their excellent traits, flavor and quick-bearing capabilities. It is to these home gardeners and their harvests that this book is dedicated.

Fabulous fruits — those delicious, juicy delights that tantalize our palates all summer long — are the focus of this book. All of these recipes can be made with minimal cooking knowledge. The dishes range from contemporary, upscale cuisine to the good country cooking that has graced our family tables for so many generations.

The fruits featured in these recipes come from the Stark Bro's trees that appear in their beautiful semiannual catalogs, and on their website (StarkBros.com). If you don't have fruit trees on your property and have the space to grow some, we hope this book might inspire you to plant a few. Experience the enjoyment and satisfaction of picking a piece of ripe, juicy fruit from your very own tree!

This blue ribbon denotes award-winning recipes submitted by Stark Bro's customers. Congratulations to our contest winners, and *bon appétit* to the readers who can now enjoy these exceptional recipes.

Mural by John Stoeckley

Foreword

For home orchard enthusiasts, the perennial dilemma is: "What on earth do I do with all of this fruit?" Immediately thereafter, the question is: "And why isn't there a good, all-around cookbook that shows me what to do with all of this fruit?"

As we celebrate our 200th anniversary as the world's oldest fruit-tree nursery (in business since 1816), we thought it was about time to fill that void. We asked the widely-published food writer and chef of the Eagle's Nest Winery & Bakery, Karen Mitcham-Stoeckley, to write one for us.

Fabulous Fruits showcases fruit in every course, from appetizers to entrées, and, most certainly, desserts. Precious few cookbooks put fruit out front; it's usually relegated to the sweets chapter at the end, or appears as a beverage-garnish afterthought. This book is an authoritative compendium of fruit-forward recipes, some elevating humble apples to new heights, and some introducing fruits like deliciously nutrition-dense goji berries to the uninitiated. All of these recipes call for fruits that can be home-grown from the wide variety of trees and plants we carry at Stark Bro's.

Karen's praiseworthy work covers the preparation of all manner of orchard fruit for all manner of courses; some classic, some adventurous, and many with a dusting of Provençal influence. The well-travelled francophile in Karen has influenced these recipes, which sparkle with simplicity — putting perfect, ripe fruit atop a pedestal and complementing it only with that which will make it taste even better. My favorite home orchard crop, peaches, are featured in a zippy salsa; I'd also recommend the contemporary pairing of chicken and Asian pears in a summer kabob recipe. It's an unexpected diversion down a culinary back road I'd never travelled... and it got me thinking about the myriad of possibilities for fruit in savory recipes, and how Stark Bro's could create new varieties to suit evolving tastes for the next 200 years.

A note about the photos: a cookbook with plain text simply instructs; a cookbook with food photographs so realistic you swear you can smell their wafting aromas, is downright transcendent. Curt Dennison's keen eye for composition results in fine-art photos that tempt, inspire and declare that it must certainly be "time to eat!"

If it is in your heart and soul to grow fruit, and then transform it into delicious things to eat, or preserve its remarkable natural beauty and flavor, this book is a mandatory addition to your cookbook collection.

Cameron Brown

President & CEO, Stark Bro's Nurseries & Orchards Co.

Appetizers, Snacks & Beverages

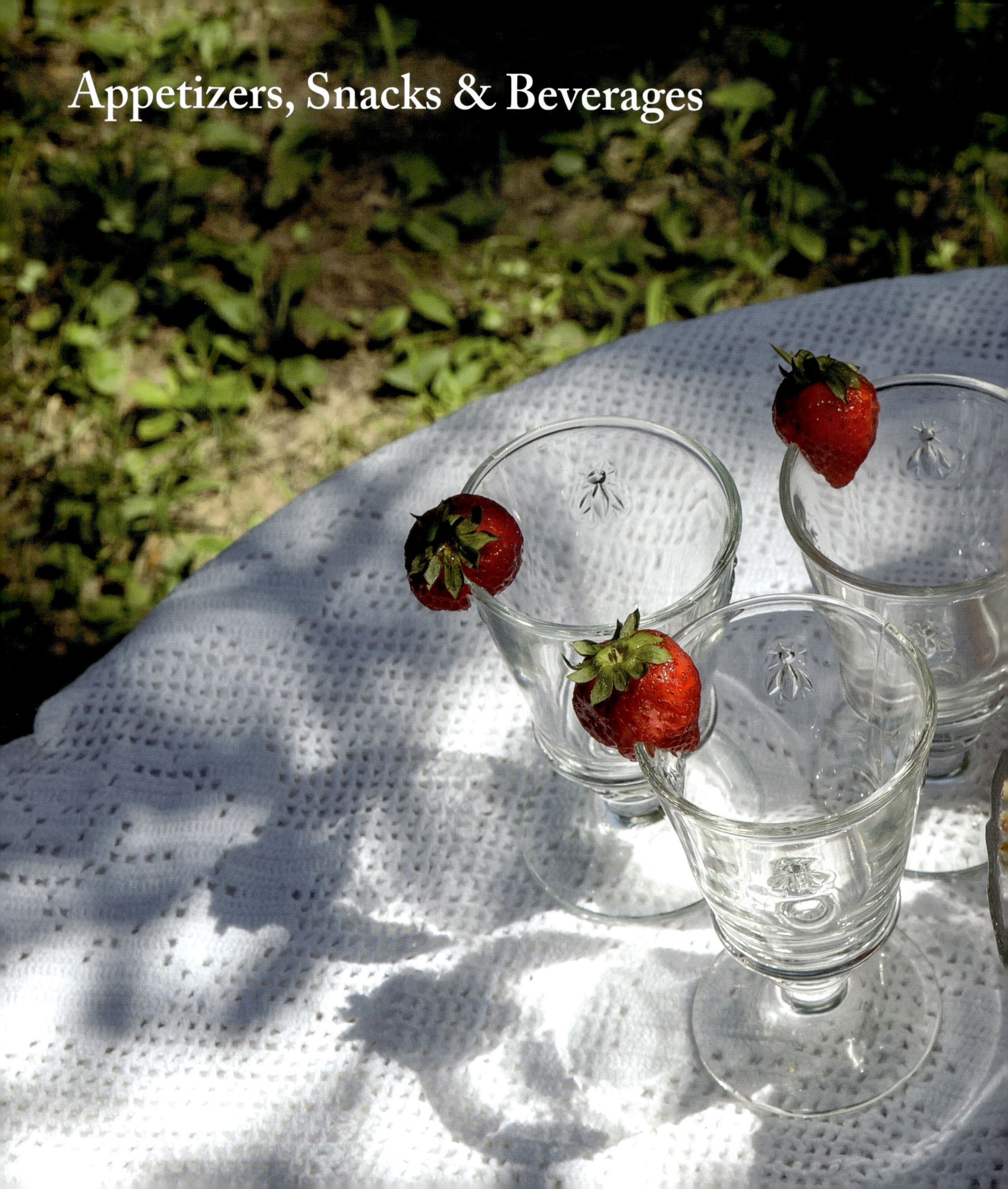

Plum Tart w/ Goat Cheese, page 26

Asian Pear, Fig & Goat Cheese Pizza

This delicious "pizza" was submitted by Melissa England from Leesburg, Virginia. It is a very tasty and unusual starter, and well-deserving of First Place in the Appetizer category. Melissa suggested using either fig, apple or pear, but we combined pears and figs for a robust flavor and texture. In a hurry? Use a prepared thin pizza crust.

Crust:
1 TBS. active dry yeast
2 cups lukewarm water (105-115 degrees)
1 TBS. honey
2 TBS. olive oil
2 tsp. sea salt
4 cups whole-wheat flour

Toppings:
1 TBS. olive oil
2 large sweet white onions, thinly sliced
2 Asian pears, peeled, thinly sliced
3 TBS. balsamic vinegar
6 large fresh figs OR 6 dried figs, soaked in warm water for 15 minutes, thinly sliced
½ cup goat cheese, crumbled (4 oz.)
1 TBS. fresh thyme leaves
20 small fresh basil leaves

- When ready to bake, preheat oven to 425 degrees.
- Pour 1 cup of lukewarm water into a large bowl and sprinkle with the yeast. Set aside for 5 minutes to foam.
- Stir honey, oil and salt into the yeast mixture.
- Gradually add the second cup of the water with the flour and stir until a sticky ball forms.
- Move the dough to an oiled bowl and lightly brush top with oil.
- Cover the bowl with a damp cloth and set aside in a warm place until dough has doubled in size, about 1 hour.
- Move the dough to a lightly floured surface and gently knead a few times to a smooth dough texture.
- In a large skillet over medium heat, heat the olive oil.
- Add the onions and stir until they turn a light brown and are translucent.
- Add the balsamic vinegar and continue to cook until the vinegar has been absorbed; set aside to cool slightly.
- Stretch the dough thin on a 12-inch pizza stone.
- Pre-bake crust for 15 minutes and remove from oven.
- Brush the pizza with the olive oil evenly.
- Top with the caramelized onions and then the crumbled goat cheese.
- Arrange the fig and apple slices over the onions and sprinkle all over with the thyme.
- Bake the pizza for 15 to 20 minutes until the cheese begins to brown.
- Remove from the oven and immediately add the basil leaves. Cut and serve.

Serves 4 as an appetizer.

Blueberry Frosty

Perfect for a quick breakfast drink or a refreshing pick-me-up in the afternoon.

1 cup ripe blueberries, stemmed and washed
2 cups plain yogurt
8–10 ice cubes
⅓ cup honey

• Place all ingredients in a blender and blend until smooth and semi-frozen.

www.starkbros.com
Everything you need in one place!

Blue Cheese & Grape Crostini

If you like blue cheese and balsamic vinegar, you'll love this tasty appetizer. So easy to prepare, and your guests will come back for seconds ... and thirds. We used tiny Champagne grapes in the photo, but any red grapes will do just fine. If they are too big, slice them in half.

2 cups seedless red grapes
3 TBS. good-quality balsamic vinegar
2 TBS. shallots, minced
3 tsp. extra-virgin olive oil
1 tsp. light brown sugar
¼ tsp. salt
1 French bread baguette, sliced diagonally into about 15 slices
(select a baguette that is crisp on the outside, not soft and spongy)
3-4 TBS. butter, softened
3 oz. crumbled blue cheese (room temperature)
½ cup toasted pecans, roughly chopped
1 TBS. fresh thyme leaves

- Preheat oven to 400 degrees.
- In a baking dish, mix together the grapes, vinegar, shallots, olive oil, brown sugar and salt.
- Gently stir to cover grapes with all the ingredients.
- Bake 20 to 25 minutes until the grapes are soft and a nice liquid forms in the bottom of the pan. Leave the oven on. (OR place these ingredients in a large non-stick skillet and sauté over a medium heat, gently stirring, for 15 minutes.)
- Place the bread slices on a cookie sheet and bake until lightly toasted. You may need to turn each piece after a few minutes, with tongs. Remove and cool slightly.
- Mix the cheese and the softened butter, and spread evenly over the bread slices.
- Return to the hot oven and bake 3 to 4 minutes, until bubbly.
- Spoon the grape mixture over the bread slices, then sprinkle with the pecans and the thyme.

Serve immediately.

Dried Snacking Apples

These delicious little apple bites make a wonderful lunchbox snack or addition to a homemade trail mix. The slices can be reconstituted by soaking them in water mixed with a squeeze of lemon juice until they soften and slightly puff up. Perfect for tarts and quick breads, the flavor is intense and the apples bake well. For a quick fruit bread with some punch, soak the apples in Calvados (apple brandy), and then use the brandy in the bread or in muffins (just not too much)!

4 lbs. apples, peeled, cored and sliced in rounds ⅛-inch thick
1 quart of ice water with 2 TBS. lemon juice added
2 cups sugar
1 cup light brown sugar
1 tsp. ground cloves
2 tsp. ground cinnamon

- Soak the apples in the lemon water for 5 minutes and drain very well.
- Mix the sugars and spices together well in a large bowl.
- Toss the apple slices gently in the sugar mixture until well coated.
- Place slices in dehydrator at 135 degrees for 12 hours. Turn all slices over and continue to dehydrate for another 12 hours.
- Apples are dried when somewhat shrunk and pliable.
- Store in plastic bags or in sterilized canning jars with two-part lids.

Goji Berry Trail Mix

The goji berry was bred in 1945 at Oregon State University, but has only recently gained worldwide popularity. Good in jams and jellies, and mixed with other fruit in pies. A plant that is rather easy to grow, it will produce all summer long. Drying the berries for use year-'round is a great way to add antioxidants and fiber to your diet, plus they taste great! Here is a snack I mix up and leave on the counter to ward off hunger attacks. Make up your own with whatever dried fruit and nuts you have on hand.

1 cup dried goji berries
1 cup soy nuts
1 cup sunflower kernels
1 cup dates, chopped
1 cup pepitas (pumpkin seeds)
1 cup dried cranberries
1 cup golden raisins
1 cup salted peanuts

- Mix all ingredients together and store in a tightly-sealed container. Serve with wine or pre-dinner drinks, along with other nibbles. Great for kids' lunchboxes or as a snack on long trips.

Makes 8 cups.

Mojito à la Framboise

Translated from a French cooking magazine, this is a delightful summer drink. You can eliminate the rum if you like, and it still is lovely and refreshing.

2 limes
24 fresh raspberries
4 sprigs of fresh mint
4 standard shot glasses of golden rum
8 TBS. simple syrup (see note below)
2 cups club soda
Ice cubes to fill 4 glasses

- Place the raspberries in the bottom of the glasses, about 6 per glass.
- Place one sprig of mint in each glass.
- Squeeze ½ lime into each glass, reserving the squeezed rind.
- Place the rind in a cocktail shaker with the rum, simple syrup and ice and shake well.
- Pour into the glass.
- Add ½ cup of the club soda and more mint if desired.

Simple Syrup: Combine 2 cups water and ½ cup sugar in a saucepan. Bring to a boil and simmer for 15 minutes. Cool and store in the refrigerator, and use as needed.

Peachy Salsa

This salsa is also delicious served at room temperature over grilled fish, chicken or pork.

2 large Roma tomatoes, seeded and coarsely chopped
3 ripe peaches, peeled and coarsely chopped
6-8 green onions, finely chopped (use some green tops)
1 small can mild green chilies (hotter if you like)
1 clove garlic, minced
¾ cup fresh cilantro leaves, chopped
1 tsp. lime zest
Juice of ½ lime
½ tsp. salt
½ tsp. finely-ground pepper

• Gently toss all ingredients together in a bowl.
• Cover tightly and refrigerate 2-3 hours for flavors to blend.
• Serve with corn chips as an appetizer.

Pear Chutney

Chutney is a very old West Indian condiment that was later adopted for use in England. Originally, it was limited to being made with dark raisins and was also referred to as a relish. As the culinary arts diversified, cooks realized that chutney was delicious using other fruits. Here, I am offering a pear version. An Asian pear is a unique variation of the species, although you may use any type of pear. Choose fruit that is on the firm side; overripe pears will result in a chutney that is mushy. Any of the **Stark® Asian Pears** are good for this dish; the **Stark® Sugarsweet** pear is also excellent.

6 cups slightly underripe pears, peeled and chopped
½ lemon, seeded and finely chopped (including the peel)
1 large yellow onion, diced
2 TBS. fresh ginger, peeled and finely chopped
1 cup golden raisins
1 medium sweet red pepper, seeded and finely chopped
¼ tsp. red pepper flakes
2 ½ cups packed brown sugar
2 cups cider vinegar
2 tsp. salt
Approx. 20 whole cloves and 1 full cinnamon stick, tied in a spice bag

4 wide-mouth pint canning jars, with lids and tops, sterilized

- Place all ingredients in a non-reactive kettle and simmer over low heat for 2 hours or longer, until the mixture begins to thicken. Stir frequently to avoid scorching. When thickened, quickly bring to a boil and remove spice bag.
- Ladle into sterile jars, wipe the rims and seal. Place in a boiling water bath for 20 minutes.

Chutney is delicious on meats — especially pâté — and is the perfect partner for curries. In a cold ham or beef sandwich with a mild cheese, chutney creates a whole different flavor and keeps the meat moist.

About 4 pints

Pear Chutney Bruschetta

This yummy bruschetta will become a signature appetizer to serve to your friends and family. A complete departure from tomato-based bruschetta, the flavors of fresh pear and shallots, enhanced with the cheese and nuts, will delight even the picky eaters in your group.

8 tsp. olive oil
⅓ cup finely-chopped shallots
1-1½ cups Anjou, Bartlett, Bosc or Asian pear, peeled and finely chopped
½ cup pear nectar or apricot nectar
1⅓ cup dried apricots, finely chopped
2 TBS. sugar
1½ TBS. cider vinegar
⅛ tsp. salt
1 (3-inch) cinnamon stick
4 oz. French bread baguette, cut diagonally into 16 ¾-inch slices and toasted
8 tsp. walnuts or pecans, toasted and chopped
8 tsp. crumbled blue cheese or Gorgonzola cheese
1 TBS. fresh chives, chopped
1 tsp. fresh thyme leaves, chopped

- Heat a small saucepan over medium-high heat.
- Add olive oil to pan; swirl to coat.
- Add shallots and sauté for 2 minutes, or until soft.
- Add pears and next 6 ingredients, including the cinnamon stick; bring to a boil. Reduce heat to medium-low and cook 20 minutes, or until pears are tender and mixture thickens. (Asian pears may require a bit more simmering time.)
- Cool to room temperature. Discard cinnamon stick.
- Spoon about 1½ TBS. chutney over each baguette slice.
- Top each with ½ tsp. walnuts or pecans and ½ tsp. cheese.
- Sprinkle evenly with chopped chives and thyme.

Serve warm or at room temperature.

Plum Tart with Prosciutto, Goat Cheese & Baby Arugula

This savory and sweet tart could also be a main course for a luncheon. Be sure to use ripe, juicy plums. The **Redheart** (semi-freestone) is a good choice for this dish, as is the **Santa Rosa,** with its pretty golden flesh.

9-inch pastry crust, placed in a removable-bottom tart pan (see page 145)
1 beaten egg
1 cup heavy cream
1 tsp. salt
½ tsp. ground pepper
8 oz. goat cheese, crumbled
8 oz. prosciutto, very thinly sliced
2 TBS. honey
4-5 ripe plums, pitted (do not peel), and cut into 6 wedges each
2 cups fresh arugula, rinsed and chilled

- Preheat oven to 350 degrees when ready to bake.
- Place the pastry in the tart pan and trim to the edge by rolling the rolling pin across the top of the overhang crust, pressing against the edge of the pan. Refrigerate 1 hour.
- In a medium mixing bowl, add the eggs, cream, goat cheese, salt and pepper. Mix well and pour into the crust.
- Tear the prosciutto into small pieces and scatter over the cream mixture.
- Place the plums on top of the tart mixture in a spiral pattern, slightly overlapping the wedges.
- Drizzle the honey over the plums.
- Bake for 30 minutes, until custard is set.
- Remove and cool 5 minutes before cutting, or hold at room temperature until serving.
- Top each slice with fresh arugula. You might also sprinkle the arugula with just a small amount of olive oil and a sprinkle a few crumbles of fresh goat cheese over the top.

Serves 6.

Strawberry Lemonade

Cool, tasty and oh-so-pretty! Keep a pitcher in the refrigerator during strawberry season.

2 cups fresh strawberries, rinsed, hulled and sliced
Juice of 4 large lemons
¾ cup sugar
1 cup boiling water
1 lemon sliced in rounds, ends discarded
1 quart sparkling water or club soda

- Place the sugar in the boiling water and stir to completely dissolve; cool and refrigerate for 1 hour.
- Juice the lemons and place juice in blender.
- Place the strawberries in the blender with the sugar water.
- Purée the strawberries, leaving some small bits visible.
- Pour into serving pitcher and add the sparkling water and lemon slices.
- Serve over ice.

Makes about 2 quarts.

Breakfast, Breads & Muffins

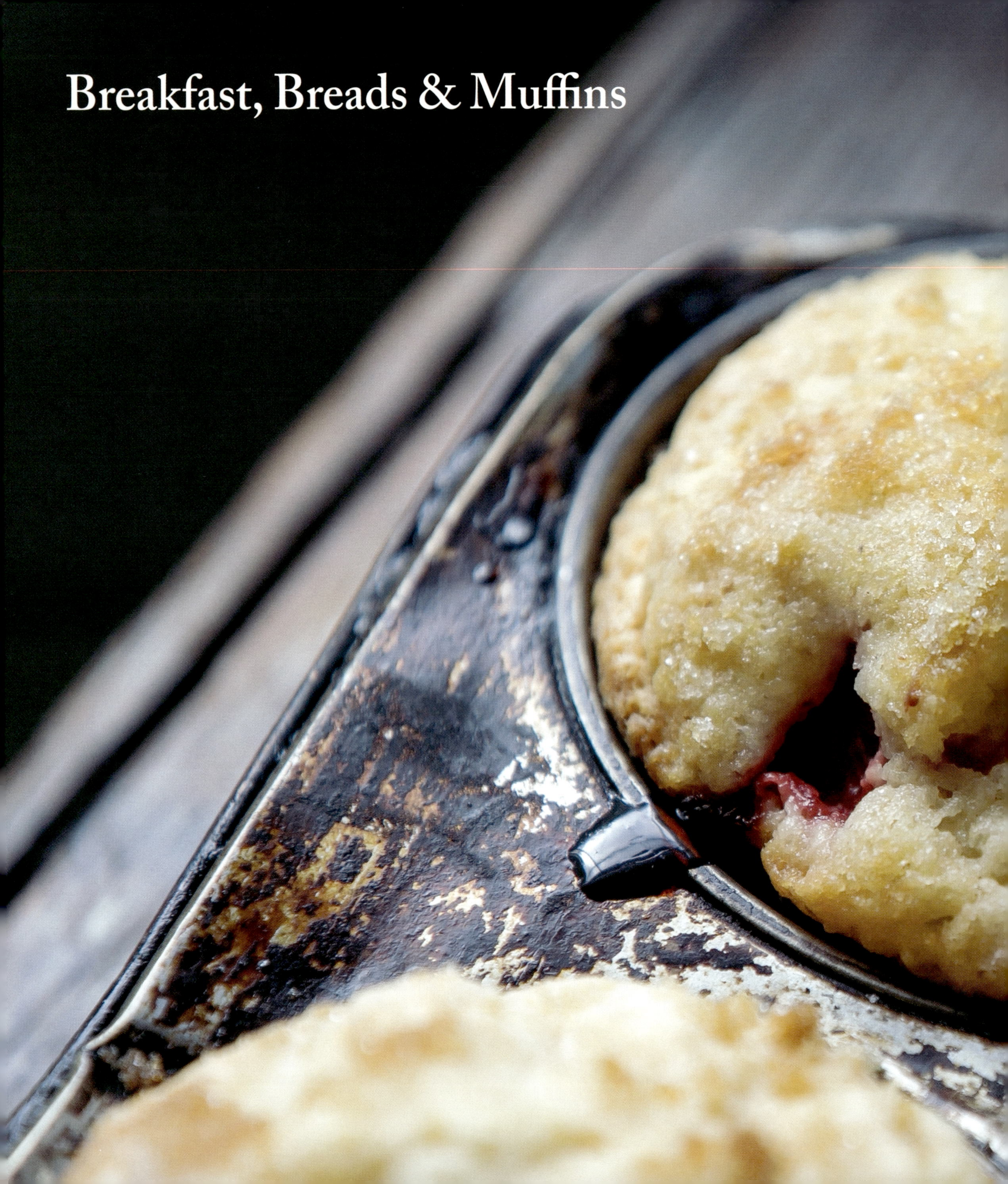

Raspberry-Ginger Muffins, page 44

Blueberry Muffins

These delicious, moist muffins can be made with raspberries, strawberries, peaches, figs or any fruit you prefer. You may also top them with a crumb topping of oatmeal, brown sugar, butter and cinnamon before baking. The recipe will make a dozen standard muffins or six jumbo-sized muffins. Serve warm as an extra treat!

2 cups all-purpose flour
1½ tsp. baking powder
¾ tsp. baking soda
½ tsp. salt
½ tsp. cinnamon
½ cup unsalted butter, softened
1 cup sour cream
⅓ cup milk
2 large eggs
1 cup fresh blueberries (or other chopped fresh fruit)

- Preheat oven to 375 degrees.
- Line muffin tin with paper baking cups.
- In a mixing bowl, combine all dry ingredients and blend well.
- In another large mixing bowl, beat butter and sugar with a mixer on medium speedy, until fluffy.
- Add the sour cream and eggs one at a time to the butter mixture, beating after the addition of each egg.
- Add the dry ingredients and the milk to the butter-sugar mixture, and blend until just combined. Do not overmix.
- Fill the muffin cups ⅔ full.
- Bake 20 minutes for standard muffins or 30 minutes for jumbo muffins. Test with a toothpick for doneness.

Blueberry Lemon Scones

This delightful award-winning recipe was sent to us by Stephanie DeLine from Cleveland Heights, Ohio. Scones are a very old traditional pastry in England and the northern islands of Europe. While many recipes are available, a moist and slightly sweet scone seems to be the favorite. I like to serve them fresh from the oven for a light luncheon instead of muffins or tea breads.

1 cup sour cream
1 tsp. baking soda
1 cup butter, softened
1 cup sugar
1 egg beaten with 1 tsp. vanilla
4 cups all-purpose bread flour
2 tsp. baking powder
¼ tsp. cream of tartar
½ tsp. salt
1 tsp. lemon extract OR 3 tsp. fresh-squeezed lemon juice
2 tsp. grated lemon rind
1 cup fresh blueberries

- Preheat oven to 350 degrees.
- Lightly grease a large baking sheet, or use parchment paper or a silicone baking mat.
- In a small bowl, combine the sour cream and baking soda and set aside.
- In a large bowl, mix the butter and sugar.
- Add the egg mixture to the butter mixture.
- Mix all the dry ingredients and add to the butter mixture.
- Add the sour cream, lemon extract and lemon zest, and gently fold in the blueberries, taking care not to smash them.
- Divide the dough into 4 balls and wrap in plastic wrap.
- Starting with the first ball, unwrap and flatten (on a lightly floured surface) into a 10-inch circle about ½-inch to ¾ thick.
- Cut the circle into 10-12 pie-shaped pieces and place on the prepared baking sheet.
- Bake 12 minutes.
- Repeat with the remaining balls of dough.
- Allow the scones to cool slightly, then glaze (below).

Glaze Layer One: 1 cup powdered sugar and 2 TBS. milk
- Mix together. Brush on the cooled scones and let dry.

Glaze Layer Two: ¼ cup melted butter, ¼ cup fresh lemon juice, 2 cups powdered sugar
- Mix together and brush over the first glazed layer, above. Let dry and serve.

Full recipe makes 40 to 48 scones. Recipe can be divided. Scones can be frozen for up to 3 months in Ziploc® bags (with the air removed to prevent freezer burn).

Breakfast Muesli

This variation of muesli from Jamie Oliver is delicious, healthy and provides a great start to any day. Kids will love it and enjoy preparing it the evening before. The fresh pear and the goji berries complement each other, but you could substitute any of your dried fruit for the goji and a fresh peach, nectarine or apricot could replace the pear.

1 cup skim milk or almond milk
1 cup quick-cooking oats (not instant)
1 TBS. shelled pumpkin seeds
2 TBS. honey
⅛ tsp. cinnamon
½ tsp. fresh lemon juice
¼ cup walnuts, coarsely chopped
2 TBS. fresh goji berries
1 ripe pear

- In a glass bowl place the oats, milk, pumpkin seeds, honey, cinnamon and lemon juice. Cover and place in the refrigerator overnight.
- In the morning, stir slightly to mix and add the walnuts and the fresh goji berries.
- Dice the pear into bite-sized pieces and top the muesli.
- If you prefer, you could add a bit more milk and heat the mix in the microwave for a quick, hot breakfast. (Don't microwave the pear.)

Cherry-Banana Bread

This lovely quick bread is wonderful with a fruit luncheon salad or on a buffet table with poultry or ham. You could substitute fresh raspberries, blueberries or honeyberries. For easy slicing, chill well first. A nice fruit bread to serve with lightly-sweetened cream cheese.

⅓ cup canola oil
½ cup sugar
2 eggs
2 cups flour
1 tsp. baking powder
½ tsp. baking soda
½ tsp. salt
½ tsp. vanilla extract
2 ripe bananas, mashed
1½ cups tart red cherries, pitted (if canned, drain well)

- Preheat oven to 350 degrees; grease and flour the bottom of a standard loaf pan.
- Place the cherries in a food processor and quick-pulse 3-4 times.
- Remove cherries to a fine sieve set over a bowl. Using a rubber spatula, press the chopped cherries to get all the juice out. Reserve ⅓ cup of juice.
- Mix oil, sugar, vanilla and eggs well with a wooden spoon.
- Mix together the dry ingredients in a separate bowl.
- Add dry ingredients to the oil mixture and mix well.
- Add the mashed banana and the chopped cherries and mix well.
- Add ⅓ cup (only) of the juice from the cherries and mix well.
- Pour the batter into the prepared loaf pan.
- Bake for 25 to 30 minutes, or until a toothpick inserted in the center comes out clean.
- Allow to cool 10 minutes on wire rack, then turn out onto a board or towel.
- Cool well before slicing. Keeps 4 days in the refrigerator wrapped in plastic wrap.

Peach French Toast Casserole

Make this casserole the night before and keep refrigerated for a quick company breakfast. You may substitute thinly-sliced apples or nectarines for the peaches.

2 cups peaches, peeled and sliced
4 TBS. butter, melted in the bottom of a 9 x 12 baking dish
4 TBS. brown sugar
1 tsp. ground cinnamon
½ tsp. ground nutmeg
1 loaf French bread, cut into ¾-inch slices
3 eggs
1½ cups whole milk
4 TBS. powdered sugar
1 tsp. vanilla
4-5 TBS. honey or maple syrup
½ cup slivered almonds

- Place the sliced peaches on top of the melted butter in the casserole.
- Sprinkle with the brown sugar, cinnamon & nutmeg.
- Evenly arrange the slices of French bread on top of the peaches.
- In a blender, mix the eggs, milk, powdered sugar and vanilla.
- Pour over the French bread, pressing down on the bread with the back of a spoon.
- Drizzle the honey or syrup on top and sprinkle with almonds.
- Allow to sit 30 minutes or overnight in the refrigerator.
- When you are ready to bake, bring the casserole to room temperature and preheat oven to 375 degrees.
- Bake 25 to 30 minutes until browned and firm to touch.
- Serve immediately with syrup or honey.

Makes 6 to 8 generous servings.

Piggy Pudding

I found this recipe in an old cookbook, written on the back of some old stationery. I do not recognize the writing, but it could be my maternal grandmother's recipe since my grandfather Denton made the best sausage in Pennsylvania! This is so simple but so good, and is a perfect breakfast casserole for the holidays and visiting family.

1 lb. of country sausage with a dash of sage
1 small box of cornbread mix
2 cooking apples, peeled, cored and sliced
3 TBS. butter, softened
½ cup maple syrup

- Preheat oven to 350 degrees.
- Brown the sausage and chop up "until a fine granule."
- Mix up the cornbread mix as per package directions.
- In an ovenproof casserole dish, place the sausage in the bottom.
- Top with the apple slices.
- Top with the corn bread mixture.
- Bake 35 to 40 minutes until corn bread is golden on top.
- Remove from oven and dot with the butter and drizzle the syrup over all.
- Serve immediately.

6 servings (maybe?)

Raspberry-Ginger Muffins

Fresh raspberries with a touch of ginger and orange make these muffins burst with flavor. When served warm, all of the flavors pop on the palate. In the winter, use the raspberries you froze during the summer.

2¼ cups flour
2½ tsp. baking powder
½ tsp. salt
½ cup sugar
¼ tsp. ground ginger
1 egg, beaten with 3 TBS. cold water
⅔ cup whole milk
1 cup fresh or frozen raspberries (if frozen, do not thaw)
⅓ cup orange juice
¼ cup unsalted butter, melted

- Preheat oven to 375 degrees. Butter 12 muffin cups or line muffin tin with paper baking cups.
- Combine the flour, baking powder, salt, ground ginger and sugar.
- Beat the egg and water together, and pour into the center of the dry mixture.
- Add the milk and gently mix together.
- Add the orange juice and blend.
- Add the melted butter and the raspberries and gently fold all together, taking care not to mash the berries.
- Ladle into buttered or sprayed muffin cups, filling each ⅔ full.
- Bake 15 minutes for standard muffins and 20-25 minutes for jumbo muffins. Test with a toothpick for doneness.

Makes 12 standard or 8 jumbo muffins.

Salads, Soups & Sides

Chicken Salad in a Peach, page 56

Apple Coleslaw

This coleslaw goes great with any wintery meal, and adds some crunch and interest to the dinner plate; mixing both green and red cabbage adds a spark of color. It holds well in the refrigerator and tastes even better the second day!

2 cups finely shredded green cabbage
2 cups finely shredded red cabbage
2 crisp apples, cored, halved and sliced (Granny Smith or Pink Lady are good choices)
½ cup canola oil
⅓ cup sugar
¼ cup red wine vinegar
½ tsp. salt

- In a large salad bowl, whisk together the oil, sugar, vinegar and salt.
- Add the shredded cabbages to the dressing.
- Add the sliced apples to the cabbage and dressing.
- Toss well to coat all with the dressing, and cover with plastic wrap.
- Refrigerate for at least 2 hours.
- Toss again before serving.

Serves 6 to 8 as a side.

Apple Kugel

Kugel is a traditional Jewish dish usually served during holidays, but is good anytime as an accompaniment for brisket, roast beef or any other main meat dish requiring a starch side. The apple pairs nicely with meat and lends a crisp contrast to the noodles. Kugel is often made with the addition of raisins; and I prefer golden raisins in this recipe.

3 large firm apples, peeled, cored and roughly chopped
1 cup unsalted butter, melted (divided)
1 TBS. kosher salt
1 lb. extra-wide egg noodles
5 large eggs
2½ cups sour cream
1 cup sugar
12 oz. cream cheese (or light cream cheese), softened
1 tsp. cinnamon
½ tsp. nutmeg

- Preheat oven to 350 degrees. Using a glass or ovenproof casserole dish that will hold approximately 8 cups, grease the bottom and sides with 1 TBS. of the butter.
- In a skillet, heat 2 TBS. of the butter over medium heat. Add 2 TBS. of sugar, cinnamon and the nutmeg. Add the apple pieces and stir to coat all with the butter and spice mix. Cook for 10 to 12 minutes, until caramelized and soft.
- Cook the noodles in boiling salted water, until just on the edge of being done. Do not overcook or the kugel will be mushy. (The noodles will continue to cook in the casserole.) Drain and place back into the pot.
- In a large bowl of an electric mixer, place the eggs and the sour cream and mix well. Add all but 2 TBS. of the sugar, ¾ cup butter and the softened cream cheese. Add the apple mixture with any syrup that is remaining. Pour this over the cooked noodles and gently fold in.
- Pour into the casserole and sprinkle the top with the 2 TBS. remaining sugar. Drizzle with an additional 2 TBS. of melted butter if desired.
- Bake for 30 minutes or until set and the top is lightly browned. Let sit for 10 minutes prior to serving to allow it to firm up.

Makes 10 – 12 servings as a side.

Baked Sweet-&-Sour Cabbage with Apples

This recipe has evolved over the years in my kitchen. It is delicious served with pork chops, roasted pork loin, roasted chicken or even fried chicken. Some folks like the fennel seed and some don't, so try it both ways to determine what your family likes best.

3 cups shredded red cabbage
3 cups shredded green cabbage
½ lb. thick-cut bacon, diced
3 apples, peeled, cored and diced
½ medium red onion, sliced
½ cup apple cider vinegar
½ cup white sugar
½ TBS. fennel seed
⅓ cup water
4 TBS. butter, cut in chunks

- Preheat oven to 350 degrees.
- Fry the bacon until almost crisp. Reserve 2 TBS. of the drippings from the bacon.
- In a large baking casserole with a lid, place the cabbage, onion and diced apple, mixing all together.
- In a small mixing bowl, whisk together the vinegar, sugar, fennel seed, reserved bacon drippings and water.
- Pour the dressing over the cabbage mixture and toss to coat everything well.
- Dot the top of the cabbage mixture with the butter chunks.
- Cover and bake 25 to 30 minutes, until the cabbage is soft.
- Gently stir before serving to bring up the juices from the bottom to coat the cabbage mixture.

Serves 6 to 8 as a side.

Blueberry Chili

Adam Dupps submitted this prize-winning recipe from Lawrenceburg, Indiana. It is certainly a different take on chili, and one that could become your family's favorite. Warm biscuits go great with this, served either as a main dish or soup course.

1 28 oz. can diced or crushed tomatoes
1 large fresh beefsteak tomato, peeled, seeded and diced
1 large sweet white onion, diced
2 cups fresh or frozen blueberries
1 lb. very lean ground beef, turkey or venison
2 TBS. ground cumin
1 tsp. cinnamon
2 tsp. paprika
1 TBS. garlic powder
1 TBS. onion powder
1 tsp. cayenne powder, or to taste
1 TBS. salt

- Do not brown meat first; simply combine all the ingredients in a large heavy-bottomed pot. Simmer over medium heat for 1 hour, until meat is fully cooked, stirring occasionally to avoid sticking.

Chicken Salad in a Peach

This recipe for chicken salad is moist and delicious, and always sure to please family and friends. A great luncheon entrée or lovely on a brunch buffet, the flavor of freshly picked sun-ripened peaches offers a dimension you will savor. A good peach for this recipe is the **Stark® Elberta Queen** or the delicious **Starking® Peach**.

Chicken Salad:
4 boneless, skinless chicken breast halves
1 cup sour cream
½ cup heavy cream
1 TBS. white vinegar
1 TBS. dried tarragon
1 cup mayo
½ cup sour cream
½ cup diced celery
1 cup red seedless grapes, halved
½ cup chopped walnuts

Peaches and side garnish:
6 ripe peaches, peeled, pitted and halved
½ cup softened cream cheese (may be light cream cheese)
2 TBS. toasted sweetened coconut
2 TBS. orange marmalade
Lettuce leaves for plating

- Preheat oven to 350 degrees.
- Mix the 1 cup of sour cream with the heavy cream and vinegar. Let sit in a warm place for 1 hour to create a sauce consistency.
- Place the chicken breasts on a lightly-sprayed jelly-roll pan or shallow baking dish and completely coat both sides with the sour cream sauce.
- Bake chicken breasts for 25 minutes or until a thermometer registers 160 degrees at the thickest point of the breast.
- Remove from oven and allow to cool completely. Scrape all the sauce and bits of browned juices into a large bowl.
- Mix in the tarragon, mayo and the ½ cup sour cream to the baked sauce.
- Chop the cooled chicken into ½-inch pieces and place into the bowl of sauce.
- Add the celery, grapes, walnuts and salt and pepper to please. Blend all well and refrigerate for two hours or overnight, covered.
- Just before serving, mix together the coconut, marmalade, and cream cheese.
- To peel the peaches: Drop the peaches in a kettle of boiling water for no more than 1 minute. Remove with a slotted spoon and place in a bowl of ice water for 4 to 5 minutes. Remove the skins and return to the ice water that now has a TBS. of lemon juice added. Remove and set on a tea towel to drain. (Do not use paper towels as they will stick to the peaches.)
- On a large platter or on individual serving plates, place lettuce leaves (Bibb lettuce lends itself well to this recipe). Cut each peach in half and remove the pit. Place 1 TBS. of the cream cheese mixture in the center of each peach half.
- Place the peach halves on the lettuce, and top with ½-¾ cup of the chicken salad.
- A nice addition to this recipe are slices of one or two of the quick fruit breads in the Breakfast, Breads & Muffins section, tucked alongside the peach on individual plates or on a separate bread tray.
- Garnish the chicken salad with red raspberries and strawberries.

Serves 6 to 8 as a buffet dish or 12 as individually-plated salads.

Homemade Applesauce

Homemade applesauce is just the best. Easy to make and delicious to eat, it tastes like fresh apples dipped in a bit of cinnamon and sugar. I like to mix two or three different types of apples together for an even fuller flavor. In my home, I serve it warm from the stove, and any leftovers are refrigerated for another meal.

*6 to 8 apples, peeled, cored and chunked (**Jonagold, McIntosh and Cortland** mix well)*
⅔ cup water
1 cinnamon stick
¼ tsp. ground nutmeg
¾ cup white sugar

- Place prepared apples in a large saucepan with the water.
- Add the cinnamon stick and nutmeg.
- Bring to a simmer over medium heat and cover.
- Slowly simmer for 20 minutes, stirring occasionally.
- When apples are soft and the water is absorbed, remove the cinnamon stick and add the sugar.
- Reduce heat to very low, but enough to let some bubbles appear. Using a potato masher, blend the apples until only a few small chunks remain, about 3 to 4 minutes of mixing with the masher.

Serves 6 as a side.

Lamb Salad with Peaches & Plums

Based on a traditional Greek dish, you will find this salad a delight as a main course or as a small-serving opener for a dinner entrée. You may use spring greens, just arugula or a mixture of your favorite greens. Other things that go well in this salad are sliced fresh figs, toasted almonds and a drizzle of honey.

1 lb. lamb, cut from the leg
3 cups arugula, kale and beet greens, rinsed well, dried and roughly chopped
1 small red onion, thinly sliced
1 large ripe peach, pitted and thinly sliced
2 ripe plums, pitted and thinly sliced
1 TBS. lemon juice
⅓ cup fresh mint leaves
½ cup light olive oil
¼ cup red wine vinegar
¼ tsp. salt
½ cup feta cheese

- Grill lamb to just medium-rare and let it rest for 10-15 minutes. Slice thinly into ½-inch strips and set aside.
- Place the chopped greens and sliced onions in a large bowl.
- In a small bowl, add the peaches and plums and drizzle the lemon juice over all. Toss gently.
- Add the fruit and sliced lamb to the greens and onions.
- In a blender place the mint, vinegar and oil and salt and purée for 1 minute.
- Drizzle the mint dressing over all, then add the feta. Toss and serve.

Serves 4 generously.

Plum, Melon & Prosciutto Salad

Quick, easy and so refreshing! This beautiful blend of summer flavors is also a treat for the eye. You can use both cantaloupe and a muskmelon, and alternate the green and orange slices.

1 ripe cantaloupe, seeded, rind removed and sliced
4 ripe plums, sliced
Red seedless grapes, halved, or tiny Champagne grapes
8-10 very thin slices of prosciutto
3-4 TBS. honey
½ cup fresh mint leaves, chopped

- On a large, round platter, begin the assembly by placing the melon slices around the outside edge in a pinwheel pattern.
- Fill in the center with slices going in the opposite direction.
- Place the plum slices on top of the melon in the opposite direction toward the center.
- Add the prosciutto around the fruit in a border between the plums and the grapes space.
- Place the grapes in the middle in a mound.
- Sprinkle the chopped mint over all.
- Drizzle the honey over everything.
- Keep chilled until ready to serve.

Red-Hot Cinnamon Apples

These beautiful apple slices will brighten up any winter meat or poultry dish. Looks and tastes great alongside the Thanksgiving turkey or holiday ham. Try the **Stark® Super Red Fuji!**

10 crisp apples, cored but not peeled
2 TBS. lemon juice
1 gallon cold water
1¾ cups sugar
1 cup red-hot cinnamon candies
1 TBS. whole cloves
2 whole cinnamon sticks
2 cups water
1 cup apple cider vinegar
1 cup light corn syrup

8 wide-mouth pint canning jars, with lids and tops, sterilized

- Slice each cored (but unpeeled) apple into round rings, about ¼-inch thick.
- In a large pan, put the gallon of water and the lemon juice. Place the apple slices in the lemon water and allow to sit until your syrup is ready.
- In a large kettle, add all of the remaining ingredients and bring to a slow boil, stirring to completely dissolve the sugar.
- Drain the apple slices well and place in the simmering syrup.
- Simmer the apples for 5 minutes, taking care not to overcook them, or they will become applesauce!
- Pack the rings in the sterilized jars, leaving headspace of about ½ inch.
- Pour the syrup into each jar and gently press down with the back of a spoon to release any air bubbles. Wipe the jar rim and top with lids.
- Place in boiling water-bath canner and process for 15 minutes. Remove and cool. Store in a cool, dark cupboard for up to 9 months.

Note, if the syrup is not red enough, you may add a few drops of red food coloring.

Makes 8 pints.

Red, White & Green Salad

This wonderful award-winning salad was submitted by Dianne Pauley from Fishers, Indiana. The flavor of roasted fresh beets and the contrast of the feta cheese bring the other ingredients to full flavor.

1 small bunch spinach leaves (about 2 cups)
Beet leaves from two or three beets, washed and torn
1 large or two medium fresh beets, baked, peeled and diced
1 large or two medium Asian pear, diced and rinsed with diluted white vinegar
½ purple onion, sliced into thin strips
½ cup crumbled feta cheese
½ cup dried goji berries
½ cup dried cherries
½ cup salted sunflower seeds

Dressing:
¼ cup seasoned rice vinegar
½ cup sesame oil
2 TBS. pure maple syrup
1 tsp. soy sauce

- Preheat oven to 350 degrees.
- Prepare beets: separate greens from the beets. Wash beets and wrap in foil.
- Bake for 40 minutes.
- Remove from oven and drop into ice water. Skins will come off easily.
- Dice beets into ¼-inch cubes.
- Layer the ingredients in the order listed.
- Combine dressing ingredients well, and pour over the salad. Gently toss and serve.

Serves 4.

Strawberry-Spinach Salad

Crisp, refreshing and delicious, this salad is a people-pleaser. Fresh strawberries from the garden bring a level of taste not usually found in a salad of this type. The **Clancy Strawberry** is a perfect berry for home-growing and this salad. This could be the whole meal with some fresh rolls and strawberry lemonade!

Salad:
8 cups baby spinach
2 cups fresh strawberries, washed, hulled and halved
½ medium red onion, thinly sliced in rounds
1 cup green grapes, halved
½ cup diced celery
½ cup golden raisins
2 TBS. toasted sunflower seeds
⅓ cup fresh basil leaves, torn into small pieces
½ cup toasted walnuts or pecans
½ cup crumbled blue cheese

Dressing:
2 TBS. red wine vinegar
4 TBS. olive oil
3 TBS. honey
¼ tsp. dry mustard
½ tsp. salt

- Place all the ingredients in a large salad bowl (except the crumbled blue cheese) and chill for at least 30 minutes.
- Place all dressing ingredients in a blender or jar with a tight lid and blend or shake until the dressing has a creamy appearance.
- Drizzle all the dressing over the salad mixture and gently toss.
- Top with blue cheese crumbles.
- Serve immediately.

Serves 8 generously.

Sweet Potatoes & Apples

This makes a wonderful fall or winter complement to any meat entrée. The onion and the bacon make this a very savory dish. Kids will like this as well as grandpa and grandma!

3 large sweet potatoes, peeled and cut into 1-inch chunks
2 cups firm baking apples, unpeeled, cored and cut into 1-inch wedges
4-5 strips thick-cut bacon, cut into 1-inch pieces
1 small yellow onion, peeled and chopped
⅓ cup half-and-half or heavy cream
Salt and pepper to taste
⅔ cup of Triscuit crackers, pulverized in a food processor
3 TBS. melted butter

- Preheat oven to 375 degrees.
- Place diced potatoes in boiling water and cook 10 minutes until still slightly firm, then drain well.
- Place the bacon in a medium skillet and cook over medium-high heat until crisp. Remove the bacon, but leave the drippings in the skillet.
- Sauté the onion in the bacon drippings.
- Put potatoes, apple wedges, onion and bacon in a buttered casserole dish. Do not clean the skillet yet.
- Place the Triscuit cracker crumbs and the melted butter in the same skillet and stir over medium-high heat for 4 minutes, until lightly browned.
- Drizzle the cream over the casserole, and salt and pepper to taste.
- Sprinkle the Triscuit crumbs over the top, and place dish in preheated oven.
- Bake for 30 minutes. If crumbs begin to get too dark, cover with foil.
- Serve hot.

Serves 6 generously as a side.

Waldorf Chicken Salad

Every Thanksgiving and Christmas, my mother made old-fashioned Waldorf Salad. Adding roasted chicken or turkey and romaine to the salad transforms it to a main dish for late supper or luncheon. It is also a great way to use up leftover turkey. I've never tried it with chopped baked ham, but I suspect that would be delicious also.

2½ lbs. whole roasted chicken or 4 cups roasted turkey
***Golden Delicious** or **CandyCrisp**® apples, unpeeled, cored and chopped*
2 stalks of celery, chopped
1 cup each seedless red and green grapes, halved
½ cup chopped walnuts
½ cup golden raisins
½ cup mayonnaise
¾ cup plain Greek yogurt
¼ cup orange juice or white grape juice
½ tsp. salt
¼ tsp. ground nutmeg
¼ tsp. cinnamon
1 small head of romaine lettuce
¼ cup chopped walnuts for top garnish

- Debone cooled chicken, removing any skin, and cut meat into bite-size pieces.
- Place chicken in a large bowl and add the apples, celery, grape halves, walnuts and raisins.
- In a small bowl, mix together the mayonnaise, yogurt, juice, salt, nutmeg and cinnamon.
- Pour the mayonnaise mixture over the chicken mixture and fold together completely.
- Chop romaine and place on a rimmed platter or in a large shallow bowl.
- Top with the chicken mixture and garnish with additional walnuts.
- Serve immediately or refrigerate.

Serves 4-6 main servings.

Main Dishes

Asian Pear & Chicken Kabobs, page 78

Apricot Chutney & Boursin Sandwich

While this apricot chutney is delicious on meat and curries, it makes a great sandwich filling for a vegetarian lunch or finger sandwiches at a cocktail party. The chutney may be made days in advance and kept refrigerated up to 1 month.

6 fresh apricots, unpeeled, pitted and chopped
½ cup golden raisins
2 medium shallots, finely minced
3 TBS. white wine vinegar
3 TBS. sugar
1 tsp. cumin
1 tsp. cinnamon
4 slices multi-grain bread (2 sandwiches)
1 package herbed Boursin cheese, room temperature
1 seedless English cucumber, thinly sliced
1 cup baby spinach leaves

- Place the first 7 ingredients in a heavy-bottom saucepan with ⅓ cup water.
- Simmer for 30 minutes until the apricots are almost in a purée state. Remove from heat and cool.
- Lightly toast the bread.
- Spread **each** slice with the soft cheese, about 2 TBS. per sandwich.
- Place about 2 TBS. of the chutney on two of the slices of toast.
- Place appropriate amount of cucumber slices on the chutney.
- Layer the spinach leaves on the cucumber and top with the other slice of toast.
- Cut on the diagonal and serve.

Makes 2 sandwiches.

Asian Pear & Chicken Kabobs

A great recipe for entertaining a large group. For a family meal, serve on flavored rice, baking a portion and freezing the rest for a future meal or a quick company appetizer. The **Asian pear** holds up nicely to cooking in this manner and adds wonderful flavor.

3 lbs. boneless chicken tenders
4 TBS. light soy sauce
½ cup brown sugar
2 tsp. ground ginger
½ cup pineapple juice or sweet white wine
2 dozen bamboo skewers, soaked in water for 1 hour
3-4 Asian pears, peeled and diced into 1-inch chunks

- Preheat the oven to 375 degrees.
- Mix the soy sauce, brown sugar, ginger and juice or wine together, using a wire whisk to blend in the ginger well.
- Cut the chicken tenders in half length-wise.
- Place the chicken tenders in a large glass baking casserole and pour the soy mixture over the tenders. Allow to marinate for 1 hour. (Do not marinate overnight as the enzymes in the pineapple juice or wine will break down the chicken cell structure.)
- Prepare the pears and soak in cold lemon water.
- Start with the end of a tender and pierce on to the skewer. Then add a pear piece, folding the tender over and weaving it onto the skewer. Repeat this so the tender is woven in and out between at least three pieces of pear per skewer. Place the skewers in a glass baking dish big enough to hold about 20 skewers. Do not crowd too close together. Use a second dish if necessary to bake the entire recipe.
- Pour any marinade over the finished skewers. Cover with foil.
- Bake in for 20 minutes. Remove foil and turn up the oven to 450 degrees. Bake for 4 or 5 more minutes to lightly brown the chicken. Do not over-bake or the chicken will dry out. Place on a platter and drizzle any of the cooked marinade juice over all.

Serves 15 to 20 as an appetizer, or 10 to 12 as a dinner entrée.

Country Ribs with Cherry BBQ Sauce

Sweet cherries and the grill make great partners. You could use this sauce on ribs, chicken or beef, but the thick, juicy country-style ribs are my favorite. If you grow and can cherries, be sure to use them and mash them up in the sauce.

3 TBS. tomato ketchup
¾ cup brown sugar
2 TBS. white wine vinegar
1 TBS. dark molasses
1 tsp. grated fresh ginger
1 TBS. Dijon mustard
2 TBS. Sweet Honey Catalina salad dressing
¾ cup tart red cherries
2 lbs. country-style ribs

Spice Rub:
½ tsp. salt
¼ tsp. pepper
½ tsp. paprika
½ tsp. garlic powder

- Rub ribs on all sides with the spice rub and set aside for 1 hour.
- Prepare a charcoal or gas grill to cook the ribs.
- Mix the first 8 ingredients together in a small saucepan and simmer over low heat for 20 minutes.
- Place ribs on a hot grill using indirect heat, avoiding flame. Close lid and grill for 10 minutes. Turn ribs and continue grilling for another 5 minutes.
- Place ribs on platter and pour the hot BBQ sauce over the ribs.

Serve 4.

Chicken Glazed with Plum Sauce

This is a delicious and tantalizing dish that blends many different flavors together. For two people, this dish will divide and freeze well for a future meal when time is short. As always, use a firm, but ripe, juicy plum. Nectarines can be used in this dish with good results.

1 lb. firm but ripe plums, pitted and chopped in small pieces
3 TBS. unsalted butter
1 yellow onion, finely minced
⅓ cup honey
2-3 TBS. water
3 TBS. purchased sweet chili sauce (in the Asian food section)
2 TBS. light soy sauce
2 tsp. finely grated fresh ginger
1 TBS. lemon zest
3 TBS. fresh lemon juice
6 skinless, boneless chicken thighs or breast halves

- Preheat the oven to 350 degrees.
- Using a food processor, purée the plums, honey and water until very smooth.
- Melt the butter in a large skillet. Add the onion and sauté for 3 minutes, until translucent. Add the purée, sweet chili sauce, soy sauce, ginger, lemon zest and juice.
- Cook, stirring gently for 5 to 7 minutes until slightly thickened.
- Season the chicken with salt and pepper, and place in a buttered oven-proof casserole or baker. Spoon the sauce over the chicken pieces.
- Bake at 350 degrees for 25 to 30 minutes, basting with the sauce every 10 minutes and turning the chicken at least once in the sauce. Bake for another 10 to 15 minutes until chicken is tender and cooked until a meat thermometer registers an internal temperature of 175 degrees.
- Serve with rice cooked in coconut milk and a pinch of grated ginger.

Serves 6.

Country Ham with White Peaches & Rosemary

This unusual entrée is the Main Dishes winner from the kitchen of Anna Bendiksen of Fairfield, Connecticut. Anna created this dish to serve on a hot summer day with her homemade biscuits. The use of the white peaches makes this dish extra-delicious, and the rosemary brings out the taste of summer, beautifully complementing the country ham. The **Stark® Saturn** donut peach works very well in this dish. Also the **Stark® Early White Giant** is a good choice; just a bit juicier.

8 white peaches (6 if using the Early White Giant), unpeeled and thinly sliced
1 lb. country ham, cut into thin strips
1-2 sprigs fresh rosemary

- Strip the leaves from the rosemary stems.
- Place the rosemary leaves in a plastic bag and crush them with a rolling pin, or chop finely with a chef's knife.
- In a large mixing bowl, combine all the ingredients along with a sprinkling of salt and fresh ground pepper.
- Serve immediately as a plated luncheon entrée.

Serves 4.

Curried Chicken with Apples

This East-Indian style dish can also be made with shrimp, pork or beef. If curry is a favorite of yours, feel free to adjust the amount of curry to intensify the flavor. I use part chicken stock when cooking rice to serve with this dish. Sometimes I use coconut milk for a sweeter taste, especially when using shrimp.

2 TBS. olive oil
2 TBS. unsalted butter
2 cups boneless cubed chicken (raw)
1 medium yellow or white onion, roughly chopped
1-2 large garlic cloves, minced
2 cups unpeeled apple, chopped into ½-inch chunks
½ cup diced sweet red pepper
½ cup golden raisins
1 TBS. curry powder, or more to taste
3 TBS. flour
2½ cups chicken stock
Salt and pepper to taste
1½ cups whole milk or half-and-half
2 TBS. chopped fresh parsley

Enough cooked rice for 4 servings

- Melt the butter with the olive oil in a large heavy-bottomed pan over medium-high heat.
- Add the cubed chicken, and stir until golden-brown, about 5 minutes.
- Add the onion, garlic, apples, red pepper, raisins and curry, and stir until tender, about 8 to 10 minutes.
- Add the flour and continue stirring for 4 to 5 minutes.
- Add the chicken stock and stir over a simmering heat for 4 to 5 minutes.
- Add salt, pepper and the milk, and continue simmering over low heat for 5 minutes. Taste for seasoning.
- On a large platter, form a rice ring with the cooked rice of choice, leaving space in the center. Spoon in the curry and sprinkle the fresh parsley all over. Serve with various condiments in separate small bowls to be passed with the curry. Good choices are: Chutney, shredded coconut, chopped peanuts, currants or raisins, bacon bits, diced hot peppers or chopped chives. I usually use 4 condiments, always a chutney.

Serves 4 generously

Grape & Lemon-Shrimp Salad

Bringing together the flavors of the fruit and the shrimp make this tasty dish perfect for friends and family meals. From start to serving, it only takes 15 to 20 minutes to prepare, making it a super weekday meal for family. Seedless red grapes could also be used.

1½ lbs. shell-on shrimp, uncooked, deveined (26-30 count)
3 cups boiling salted water
1 cup couscous
1 cup water from the shrimp boil
½ lb. fresh sugar snap peas, strings removed and cut into 1-inch pieces
1 cup seedless green grapes, halved
3 TBS. green onion with tops, thinly sliced
½ cup fresh basil, torn in small pieces
2 TBS. grapeseed oil
2 tsp. lemon zest
2 TBS. fresh lemon juice
¾ tsp. salt
¼ tsp. ground pepper

- To the rapidly-boiling salted water, add shrimp all at once. Remove from heat and let sit for exactly 3 minutes. Drain the shrimp, reserving 1 cup of the water. Cool and peel the shrimp.
- Place couscous in a large bowl.
- Add the 1 cup of hot shrimp water and a pinch each of salt and pepper.
- Cover for 5 minutes and then fluff with a fork.
- In a large bowl, combine the pea pods, onion, lemon zest, juice, shrimp, grapes, basil, oil, and ¾ tsp. salt and ¼ tsp. pepper and toss well.
- Place couscous on large platter and spoon shrimp mixture over the top.
- Serve immediately.

Serves 4 to 6

Lamb Loin Chops with Blackberry Sauce

This heavenly entrée was submitted by Eric Machamer of Commerce City, Colorado. It takes a bit of devotion to prepare, but is well worth the time for a special company dish you will be proud to serve. Double the ingredients for four servings.

4 lamb loin chops cut 2 inches thick
1 tsp. finely minced garlic
1 tsp. sea salt
¼ tsp. black pepper
1 TBS. olive oil
1 jalapeño pepper, seeded, veins removed, finely minced

1 large shallot, finely minced
1 tsp. fresh rosemary, chopped
2 cloves garlic, minced
4 oz. package fresh blackberries
1 tsp. nutmeg
1 tsp. sea salt
½ tsp. black pepper, fresh ground

- Cut the individual loin chops from a full 8-bone rack, cutting adjacent to the bone.
- French the bones about 2½ inches down from the ends.
- Rub the chops all over with the garlic and season both sides with the salt and pepper.
- Cover the chops with plastic wrap and refrigerate for 1 hour.
- Preheat a gas grill to about 450 degrees.
- Meanwhile, add the olive oil to a medium saucepan over medium heat until warm but not smoking.
- Add the jalapeño, shallot and rosemary and sauté for 2 minutes.
- Add the 2 cloves of minced garlic and sauté for 3 minutes.
- Add half of the blackberries and cook for 5 minutes more.
- Place the mixture in a blender and allow to cool. Blend until smooth.
- Strain the sauce thru a wire sieve, forcing the liquids thru with the back of a wooden spoon. Discard remaining seeds and pulp.
- Coarsely chop the remaining blackberries.
- Place the lamb chops on the grill, close the lid and cook for 90 seconds.
- Open the lid and rotate the chops 90 degrees with tongs.
- Close the grill and cook another 90 seconds.
- Repeat the grilling method on the other side of the chops.
- Remove the chops to a warm platter and let rest 5 minutes.
- Bring the sauce back to a low simmer and add the chopped blackberries.
- Divide the sauce into the center of two dinner plates and serve the chops on top of the sauce, drizzling just a bit on top of the chops.
- The author suggests serving the chops with garlic mashed potatoes, a wedge of white cheddar cheese and a bright green vegetable.

NOTE: The grilling time of 3 minutes per side will produce a medium-rare chop; 4 minutes per side will produce a deeply-charred medium chop. Do not overcook the lamb or it will be tough. Traditionally, lamb is meant to be served medium-rare or medium, at most.

Mom's Brisket with Dried Fruit

This recipe came to me from a dear friend who made it many times for her husband, five children and grandchildren. It's luscious and warming, and fills the kitchen with an aroma that just does not stop! The fruit you dry in the summer comes back full-flavored in this main course. A two-day dish: prepare it one day, and chill and serve hot the next day. Perfect for Sunday dinner!

4 TBS. butter
3 large onions, roughly chopped
2 12-oz. bottles of regular beer
1 bay leaf
5 lbs. beef brisket, trimmed of all visible fat
Salt and pepper
½ cup (packed) pitted prunes
½ cup (packed) dried apricots
½ cup chopped dried apples
½ cup dried sour cherries
⅓ cup brown sugar
3 TBS. fresh lemon juice
2 TBS. brandy or Calvados
2 TBS. lemon zest
¼ tsp. ground ginger
1 cinnamon stick

- Preheat oven to 350 degrees.
- In a large, ovenproof kettle or flame-proof casserole dish, melt the butter over medium heat.
- Add the onions and sauté until lightly golden, 8 to 10 minutes.
- Stir in the beer and the bay leaf, and loosen any browned bits.
- Season the brisket with the salt, pepper and place brisket in the kettle.
- Spoon some of the liquid over the meat and bring to a simmer on the stovetop.
- Cover and place in the oven, basting frequently. Turn the meat over after 2 hours.
- Continue roasting until fork-tender, about 1½ additional hours.
- Transfer the brisket to a large plate, using two spatulas or tongs; cool.
- Cool the liquid and return the brisket to the pan, cover and refrigerate overnight.
- Discard any solid fat on the top of the cooking liquid.
- Reheat the brisket on the stovetop over medium heat until warmed through, about 30 to 40 minutes.
- Transfer the brisket to a cutting board and allow to sit 15 minutes.
- Slice across the grain about ½-inch thick, and arrange on a platter.
- Cover with foil, place in preheated 200-degree oven.
- Pour cooking liquid into a medium saucepan and place the remainder of ingredients in the saucepan. Simmer over medium-low heat until sauce has thickened, about 15 minutes.
- Discard cinnamon stick.
- Season with salt and pepper, spoon sauce over sliced brisket, and serve.

Makes 10 – 12 servings.

Peach Chicken Bake

A good way to bring the sweetness of summer peaches and savory chicken together. If you freeze or can peaches in the summer, use them for a fine winter dish, an easy weekday supper or to dress up Sunday dinner for friends and family. I also find this a good carry-in dish for potluck suppers.

4 boneless, skinless chicken breast halves
1 cup brown sugar
2 firm peaches, peeled, pitted and sliced
⅛ tsp. each ground ginger and cloves
2 TBS. fresh lemon juice

- Preheat oven to 350 degrees.
- Lightly oil the bottom of a 9 x 12 baking dish or oval baker.
- Place chicken in baking dish.
- In a small bowl, mix together the brown sugar, ginger, cloves and lemon juice.
- Sprinkle ½ of the brown sugar mixture over the chicken.
- Evenly arrange the peach slices over the top of the chicken.
- Sprinkle the remaining brown sugar mixture over the peaches.
- Bake 30-40 minutes, basting frequently, until the chicken registers 160 degrees on a meat thermometer at the thickest part.

Serves 4.

Pork Chops with Caramelized Apples

Pork and apples just go together so well that you will want to always include some apples in every pork dish you make. This sweet-and-savory quick dinner is a perfect family supper any night of the week.

4 bone-in pork chops, ¾-inch thick
4 large apples, peeled, cored and cut into wedges
2 tsp. dried thyme, crushed
1½ tsp. pepper
½ tsp. salt
6 TBS. butter
¾ cup sugar

- Pat chops dry. In small bowl, mix together thyme, pepper, and salt. Season both sides of chops, set aside.
- In a large heavy skillet melt the butter with the sugar over medium-high heat. Add apples and sauté for 3-4 minutes, until apples begin to brown. Turn the apples and cook for 5 more minutes until golden brown and sauce is thickened. Remove from heat and keep warm.
- Heat another heavy skillet over medium-high heat and brush with vegetable or olive oil. Add chops and brown on one side, about 4 minutes; turn and brown other side, about 4 minutes more. Keep turning chops every couple of minutes until done (internal temperature of 155° degrees).
- Serve chops with apples.

Makes 4 servings.

Pork Loin Cherry-Ancho

A zippy sauce with cherries makes this pork loin something very special. Easy to make, it all can be done the day ahead and held in the refrigerator until time to roast and dress.

2 TBS. canola oil
1 TBS. Dijon mustard
3 large garlic cloves, minced
1 tsp. fresh lime zest
1 TBS. fresh lime juice
1 4–5 lb. pork loin
¼ tsp. salt
¼ tsp. black pepper
½ cup finely chopped red onion
1½ tsp. ancho chile powder (or more if you want it spicier)
1 cup dark sweet cherries
1 cup cherry preserves
1 TBS. red wine vinegar
1 TBS. fresh mint leaves, chopped

- Preheat oven to 400 degrees.
- Lightly oil the bottom of a roasting pan.
- Mix together ½ of the oil, mustard, garlic, lime zest and juice.
- Place the pork loin in the roasting pan and rub all over with the mustard mixture. Season with salt and pepper.
- Roast the pork loin, uncovered, for 50 to 60 minutes.
- In a small saucepan, place the remaining oil, add the onion and sauté for 3 minutes over medium-high heat.
- Add the ancho chile powder and quickly stir into the onions.
- Immediately add the cherries and the preserves, and simmer until the preserves are melted.
- Add the vinegar. Remove from heat and add the chopped mint. Cover and set aside.
- Remove pork from the oven and tent with foil, allowing it to rest for 10 to 15 minutes.
- Slice the pork into ¼-inch thick slices.
- Place on serving platter and top with the slightly cooled cherry sauce.
- Garnish with mint.

Serves 8 as a main dish.

Pork Loin in Cider

This dish offers the perfect fall flavors for friends and family. Combining the fresh fall apple cider with cream brings together a rich flavor and taste that enhances the pork loin as well as the crisp apples. This is a real people pleaser recipe.

4 TBS. unsalted butter
3-4 sweet crisp apples cored and cut into fourths
1 TBS. sugar
1½ TBS. olive oil
2-3 lb. pork loin
2 TBS. unsalted butter
2 medium shallots, chopped
1½ cups apple cider
½ cup chicken stock
¾ cup heavy cream

- Melt the butter in a frying pan and add the apples and sugar and cook over low heat for about 5-6 minutes until the apple is slightly tender and glazed.
- In another larger frying pan heat the olive oil and sauté the loin(s) on all sides until dark golden brown about 7-8 minutes on each side, until the loin is cooked thru but not overdone.
- Remove the loin to a heated platter and tent with foil to keep warm.
- Add the two TBS. butter to the skillet and cook the shallots for 3-4 minutes but do not brown.
- Add the cider, chicken stock and cream and bring to a boil.
- Reduce heat and simmer for 10 minutes until reduced to a nice glaze.
- Season with salt and pepper to taste.
- Return the loin to the skillet and place in preheated 375 degree oven for 8-9 minutes.
- Add the apples and spoon some glaze over them.
- Serve immediately.

Serves 4

Salmon with Thai Red Curry & Plums

This sweet-and-spicy salmon is a crowd-pleaser and is also easy to prepare for just family. Just double or triple the recipe for a group party. Red curry paste, frequently used in Thai and other East Asian dishes is available in most upscale grocery stores. Choose ripe, juicy plums of a red or purple variety.

4 5-6 oz. salmon fillets
2 TBS. red curry paste
1 TBS. sesame oil
2 TBS. brown sugar
2 ripe but firm plums, sliced
½ tsp. each salt and pepper
1 cup coconut rice
2 cups chicken or veggie stock
3 green onions with tops, sliced
1 TBS. sesame oil
Chopped parsley or cilantro for garnish, optional

- Preheat oven broiler and cover a broiler pan with lightly-oiled foil.
- In a deep saucepan, place the green onions and sauté in just a dash of sesame oil for 2 minutes.
- Add the stock and the coconut rice, and bring to a boil. Cover and lower the heat to a simmer. Cook for 15 minutes until all moisture is absorbed and rice is tender. Keep covered and set aside.
- Place salmon fillets on the broiler pan.
- Mix together the red curry paste, sesame oil, brown sugar, and salt and pepper.
- Brush the salmon with ½ of the mixture and place under the broiler for 3-4 minutes.
- Remove from broiler and turn each piece over.
- Top each fillet with the plum slices and brush all with remaining paste.
- Return to broiler for 3-4 minutes until the plums begin to brown on the edges.
- Take care not to overcook the salmon. It should remain moist and light pink on the inside.
- Remove pan from oven and tent with foil to keep hot.
- Serve each fillet on top of a scoop of the coconut rice.
- Garnish with a bit of chopped cilantro or parsley.

Serves 4.

Desserts

Apricot Tart from the Alps, page 112

Apple Croustade

This recipe came to me from a chef who ran my restaurant kitchen years ago. It is a stunning dessert as well as delicious. It is a bit time-consuming, but worth every minute. Perfect for a special company dinner when you have time to make an elegant dessert. Be sure to use phyllo (sometimes spelled "filo") dough, not pastry dough. Phyllo can be a challenge to work with, but keep it covered with a damp cloth, and handle it gently.

1 package frozen phyllo dough, thawed but not opened
6 firm cooking apples, peeled and cored
1 TBS. lemon juice
12 walnut halves
12 TBS. caramel ice cream topping (divided)
½ cup sugar
1 TBS. ground cinnamon
½ cup melted butter
Vanilla ice cream for serving

- Preheat the oven to 350 degrees.
- Place the whole apples in a large saucepan with enough water to cover.
- Add the lemon juice and bring to a boil for 5 minutes. Do not overcook. Apples should be firm.
- Drain the apples well and allow to cool completely.
- Open the rectangular phyllo dough, and using kitchen scissors, cut the dough off on one end to make the dough square, saving the strips. Cover the dough with a damp dish towel.
- Mix together the sugar and cinnamon in a bowl and roll each apple in the mixture to coat.
- Using two sheets of dough, brush with the melted butter and place the apple in the middle.
- Push two walnut pieces down into the core hole and spoon in 1 TBS. caramel topping.
- Bring the sides of the phyllo up over the apple from the corners and pinch together, making a top knot.
- Repeat this process, rotating the dough by ⅓ each time under the apple, until you have 6 sheets of dough on the apple and making a complete top knot that fans out a bit.
- Using a few end strips, wrap them gently around the top knot and brush the package with melted butter and lightly sprinkle with cinnamon sugar.
- Repeat this process with each apple.
- Place on buttered parchment paper or a nonstick baking sheet and bake for 25 minutes.
- Serve with ice cream and a TBS. of caramel drizzled over the top. Do not refrigerate or the dough will wilt and become soft.

May be left out, lightly covered, for 1 day.

Apple Pudding Cake with Cinnamon-Butter Sauce

Cake:
1 cup (packed) brown sugar
¼ cup butter, softened
1 egg
1 cup flour
1 tsp. baking soda
1 tsp. ground cinnamon
½ tsp. ground nutmeg
¼ tsp. salt
2 cups peeled, chopped apples

- Heat oven to 350° degrees. Grease bottom and sides of an 8-inch square pan.
- In large bowl mix brown sugar and softened butter with a spoon until light and fluffy.
- Beat in egg.
- Stir in flour, baking soda, cinnamon, nutmeg, and salt.
- Stir in apples.
- Spread in pan.
- Bake 25-35 minutes or until toothpick inserted in center comes out clean.

Sauce:
⅓ cup butter
⅔ cup granulated sugar
⅓ cup half-and-half
1 tsp. ground cinnamon

- In 1-quart saucepan, heat sauce ingredients over medium heat, stirring frequently until butter is melted and sauce is hot.
- Serve warm sauce over warm cake.

Makes 8-10 servings.

Apricot-Almond Upside-Down Cake

A step above the traditional pineapple upside-down cake, this apricot version is not only delicious, but quite pretty. Included here is a traditional yellow cake recipe, but if you are in a hurry, don't hesitate to use a good-quality yellow cake mix.

6 fresh ripe apricots, peeled, pitted and halved
1 stick unsalted butter
1 cup light brown sugar
⅓ cup slivered almonds
2½ cups all-purpose flour
1⅓ cups sugar
½ cup soft butter
1¼ cups whole milk
4 tsp. baking powder
1 tsp. salt
1 tsp. vanilla
3 eggs

- Preheat oven to 350 degrees.
- Mix together all the cake ingredients in a mixer bowl.
- Beat on medium speed for 3 minutes, until all ingredients are well-blended.
- Set cake mixture aside.
- In a large deep nonstick ovenproof skillet, melt the stick of butter.
- Add the brown sugar and simmer until bubbly.
- Sprinkle the almonds evenly over the skillet.
- Place the prepared apricot halves, cut side UP in the skillet in an attractive pattern.
- Cook over low heat for 5 minutes to slightly caramelize the apricots.
- Carefully and evenly pour the cake mixture over the apricots.
- Bake for 40-45 minutes, until the top springs back when lightly pressed.
- Immediately invert onto a serving plate: Using a round plate at least two inches larger than the skillet, place plate on top of the of the skillet and using heavy tea towels to hold the plate and skillet together, invert so the cake drops onto the plate.
- Slice and serve with fresh whipped cream.

Makes 8 servings.

Apricot Tart From the Alps

This tart is a traditional Swiss or German tart, and is the reason you bought that removable-bottom tart pan at the kitchen party three years ago! By baking in a tart pan, it will allow removal for a nicer presentation as well as ease in slicing. Fresh **Stark® Sweetheart Apricots** are perfect for this dessert. An added benefit is the "almond" in the center of the pit that can be used in the filling. *Do not use the center of a pit from any other apricot as they are not edible.*

Pastry for a 10-inch tart:
1¼ cups flour
1 stick plus 1 TBS. butter, softened
4 TBS. superfine sugar or vanilla sugar

- Preheat the oven to 425 degrees.
- In a stand mixer or with a hand-held mixer, blend the sugar and butter until creamy and lemon-colored, about 5 minutes. Add the flour in small additions and continue to blend well. The dough will become thick and when the mixer strains, stop and blend with a wooden spoon or your clean hands.
- Press the dough into the tart pan pushing it up the sides to fill the sides to the very top of the edges. Do not allow to hang over the edge. Chill for 1 hour.
- Place baking beads or dried beans in the shell completely up the sides and across the bottom.
- Bake for 10 to 12 minutes. Remove and allow to cool before removing beads.

Filling:
8 oz. cream cheese (or light cream cheese)
⅓ cup superfine sugar or vanilla sugar
Zest of 1 medium orange
Zest of 1 small lemon
1 large egg
5 fresh apricots, peeled, pitted and halved
⅓ cup toasted apricot pit almonds or a mixture of almonds and the pit almond
¼ cup of cinnamon sugar

- Chop the almonds/pit almonds and toast for 8 minutes in a 375-degree oven, stirring a few times.
- In a mixer blend together the cream cheese, sugar and the citrus zests. Add the egg and mix well, about 4 minutes.
- Pour the mixture into the cooled pastry shell.
- Place the apricot halves, cut side down, on top of the cream-cheese mixture.
- Evenly sprinkle the toasted almonds over the apricots and sprinkle with the cinnamon sugar.

Serves 8.

Baked Honey Apples with Sweet Cream

The aroma of baking apples in honey and cinnamon makes the whole house feel cozy and welcoming. The **Stark® GrandGala™** apple is perfect for this dessert.
The raisins can be replaced with finely-chopped candied ginger or chopped dried apricots.

4 baking apples, cored but not cut through the bottom, peel top third from stem-end
¼ cup brown sugar
⅓ cup honey
½ tsp. cinnamon
¼ tsp. ground nutmeg
4 TBS. golden raisins (or other fruit)
4 TBS. cold butter, cut into 4 equal pieces
¼ cup apple juice or sweet white wine
½ cup heavy cream
¼ cup honey

- Preheat oven to 350 degrees.
- Place apples in a baking dish or in individual apple bakers with a TBS. of butter under each apple.
- Stuff center with raisins or other fruit.
- Mix together the brown sugar, honey, spices and juice.
- Pour mixture evenly over apples.
- Tent with foil and place in preheated oven. Bake 50-60 minutes, basting occasionally.
- Uncover and bake 10 additional minutes. Remove from oven.
- Heat the cream (do not boil), add the honey and serve with the apples.

Serves 4.

Blackberry Ricotta Cake

Perfect for a weekday dessert or as a warm coffee cake on Sunday morning. The cake can be made 1 or 2 days in advance and held at room temperature, tightly wrapped in plastic wrap.

1½ cups flour
1 cup sugar
2 tsp. baking powder
½ tsp. salt
3 large or 4 medium eggs
1½ cups low-fat ricotta cheese
½ tsp. almond extract
1 stick butter, melted
1½ cups fresh blackberries

- Preheat oven to 350 degrees.
- Line a 9-inch round cake pan with a piece of baking parchment cut to fit the bottom. Spray the parchment with vegetable spray.
- Blend together the dry ingredients in a large bowl.
- In a separate bowl, beat the eggs and ricotta together, and add the almond extract.
- Fold the ricotta mixture into the dry ingredients.
- Add the melted butter and ½ of the berries. Blend well but take care not to mash the berries.
- Pour batter into the cake pan and top with the remaining berries.
- Bake 50 to 60 minutes, testing with a toothpick for doneness.
- Cool on wire rack for 15 minutes before unmolding on to a serving platter.

Makes 6 to 8 nice servings. Top with whipped cream, if desired.

Blueberry Gâteau

This cake is very much like a French clafouti, which calls for sweet dark cherries. For some unknown reason, the old clafouti recipes used unpitted cherries, which I do not recommend! In any case this gâteau (French for "cake") can be made with sweet dark PITTED cherries, or blueberries. A nice dollop of whipped cream with some lemon zest (folded in at the very last of whipping), adds another yummy flavor.

1 cup plus 1 tsp. flour
1 tsp. baking powder
⅛ tsp. salt
½ cup unsalted butter
1 cup plus 1 TBS. sugar
2 large eggs
2½ cups blueberries, rinsed and drained (thawed if frozen)
½ tsp. lemon juice
1 TBS. powdered sugar

- Preheat oven to 350 degrees. Grease and flour a 9-inch springform pan. Set aside.
- In medium mixing bowl, sift together 1 cup flour, baking powder and salt. Set aside.
- Using a mixer on medium speed, beat butter and 1 cup sugar until light and fluffy.
- Add eggs, one at a time, and beat until blended.
- Reduce mixer speed to low and gradually add flour mixture. Beat until just incorporated.
- Spread batter evenly into prepared pan.
- In medium bowl, toss blueberries with remaining flour, sugar and lemon juice.
- Spoon berries evenly over batter.
- Bake on middle rack of oven until toothpick inserted in center comes out clean, about 45 minutes. Take care not to overbake or your cake will be very dry. Cool in pan on wire rack. Use a knife to loosen cake from sides of pan and release cake from the springform.
- Transfer to a plate, berry side up, sprinkle with powdered sugar (if desired). Serve warm or at room temperature.

Makes 8 servings.

Blueberry & Peach Pie

Mixing these two popular fruits together creates a melody of flavors that shout "summer!" When blind-baking, you may use pie weights or dried beans. I have used the same beans for years, storing them in a quart canning jar after they have cooled.

Crust:
Prepare your favorite crust recipe or use pre-made frozen crusts, thawed. Blind-bake bottom crust for 12 minutes and cut lattice strips for the top.

Filling:
2 cups blueberries, rinsed and drained (thawed if frozen)
3 cups fresh peaches, peeled, pitted and sliced
¾ cup sugar
3 TBS. cornstarch
½ tsp. cinnamon
½ tsp. grated lemon zest
1 large egg, lightly beaten
1 TBS. sugar

- Place blueberries and peaches in large bowl.
- In a small bowl, combine sugar, cornstarch, cinnamon and lemon zest.
- Add sugar mixture to blueberries and peaches and gently toss to coat.
- Spoon the fruit filling into baked crust.
- Place dough strips on top of filling in a crisscross pattern to form a lattice. Trim ends, leaving a ½ inch overhang, and crimp the edges.
- Lightly brush the lattice with beaten egg and sprinkle with sugar. Loosely cover the crimped edge of crust with a foil collar to prevent over-browning.
- Place pie on middle rack of oven and bake until filling bubbles and crust is golden brown, about 45 minutes.
- Cool on wire rack.
- Serve at room temperature.

Makes 1 10-inch pie.

Bread Pudding with Goji Berries

Looking for creative ways to use goji berries other than just as a good snack, I tried them in bread pudding with an apple. Soaking dried gojis in a little Calvados for about ½ hour plumped them up and added another great taste to the pudding. It's important to know that goji berries have some of the highest antioxidant content of any food, and are high in fiber and vitamins as well.

½ cup dried goji berries
⅓ cup Calvados (apple brandy)
2 TBS. melted butter
4 eggs, well beaten
⅓ cup brown sugar
⅓ cup white sugar
½ tsp. vanilla
1⅓ cups whole milk
1 apple, unpeeled, cored and diced
1 large loaf of stale French bread, torn into bite-sized pieces
⅓ stick butter, cut into bits

- When ready to bake, preheat oven to 350 degrees.
- Place the goji berries in the Calvados, and set aside to soften.
- Pour the melted butter into a 6- to 8-cup baking dish.
- Mix the eggs with both sugars and the vanilla, whisking well.
- Add the milk and blend completely.
- Add the gojis, Calvados and the apple pieces and mix well.
- Place the torn bread in the casserole.
- Pour the mixture over the bread and gently toss to coat well with the egg mixture. Dot the top with the bits of butter.
- Cover with foil and allow to sit in the refrigerator for 2 hours, or overnight.
- Bake, covered, for 25 minutes in the preheated oven.
- Uncover and bake 15 more minutes, until the top is golden brown.
- Serve hot or at room temperature. You may complement each serving with whipped cream.

Serves 6 generously.

Caramelized Peaches in Crêpes

You will love this simple-yet-elegant, delicious dessert. The rosemary brings a nice savory flavor to the sweet peaches and whipped cream. By purchasing ready-made crêpes, you do very little preparation and get lots of reward!

½ cup sugar
½ tsp. coarse salt
¼ tsp. ground cinnamon
8 fresh peaches, peeled, pitted and cut into 2-inch thick wedges
⅓ cup brandy or Cognac
4 TBS. unsalted butter
⅓ cup heavy cream
12 10-inch crêpes
1 tsp. chopped rosemary and 1 small sprig rosemary, for garnish, per serving

Whipped cream, for garnish

- Combine sugar, salt and cinnamon in a large bowl.
- Add peaches and toss to coat well.
- Heat a large skillet over medium-high heat.
- Place peaches in skillet and sprinkle with remaining sugar and cinnamon.
- Cook, turning peaches after 5 minutes. Continue cooking until sugar caramelizes and peaches are tender, about 2-3 additional minutes.
- Add brandy and cook until reduced, about 2 minutes.
- Add butter and cream, swirling to melt butter and combine. Cook until thick, about 2 minutes.
- Place a crêpe on a plate, and spoon the peaches into the center. Fold the crepe over the peaches like an envelope, with the peaches peeking out one end. Garnish with fresh whipped cream with just a touch or almond flavoring (optional). A fresh sprig of rosemary tucked into the whipped cream makes a lovely presentation.

Makes 12 medium crêpes.

Raspberry-Chocolate Bake

Using dark chocolate makes this dessert extra-delicious and adds a depth that milk chocolate can't. In the winter months, you may use frozen raspberries. Serve it hot or room temperature topped with some Chantilly cream or, in the summer, with vanilla ice cream.

Topping:
½ cup wheat pastry flour or almond flour or white pastry flour
½ cup quick-cooking oats
1 TBS. canola oil or coconut oil
¼ tsp. salt
2 TBS. good maple syrup

Filling:
2½ cups fresh raspberries
1½ tsp. cornstarch
½ tsp. almond extract
3 TBS. dark chocolate chips

- Preheat oven to 350 degrees.
- Lightly butter 4 six-oz. or 6 four-oz. baking ramekins. Place ramekins on a rimmed cookie sheet and set aside.
- Gently mix the ingredients for the filling and set aside.
- Place the oats, salt and flour in the bowl of a food processor with the steel blade and pulse for 30 seconds.
- Add the oil, syrup and extract and pulse 30 more seconds, until mixture begins to lump together.
- Divide the fruit mixture evenly amongst the ramekins.
- Divide the crumb mixture evenly over top the raspberry mixture.
- Bake for 25 to 30 minutes, until top is lightly browned.

Serves 4 or 6.

If serving the same day as baking, do not refrigerate; serve warm or at room temperature. If serving the next day, cover with plastic wrap and refrigerate. Place in preheated 350-degree oven for 8 minutes to reheat before serving.

Classic American Apple Pie

This recipe is a throwback to the early days of America, and is about as basic and delicious as any recipe around.

Pastry for a two-crust 9-inch pie (see page 145)

5 large apples, peeled, cored and cut into ½-inch slices
½ cup sugar
2 TBS. all-purpose flour
½ tsp. cinnamon
¼ tsp. nutmeg OR allspice
2 TBS. cold butter, cut into small pieces
1 TBS. milk
2 TBS. sugar, divided

- Preheat the oven to 375 degrees.
- Roll out pie dough and place in the bottom of the pie plate, leaving some overhang.
- In a large bowl, combine the apples, 1 TBS. sugar, flour, spices and the butter pieces. Gently mix until the apples are well-coated.
- Place apple mixture in the crust.
- Roll out the top crust to about 10 inches in diameter and cut a small design in the middle of the crust.
- Fold the dough in half and lift to the pie, center it and unfold.
- Crimp around the edges, sealing together the lower crust and the top crust.
- Brush the top with the milk and sprinkle with 1 TBS. of sugar.
- Place in the middle of the preheated oven and bake for 50-60 minutes. If crust browns on the edges too soon, cover with aluminum foil strips. Do not cover the top.
- Remove and allow to cool before cutting.

8 servings.

Fresh Apple Cake

My little sister Susan gave me this recipe, and it is a real winner. The Browned-Butter Frosting brings a whole different flavor to a standard apple cake. Great for family gatherings, carry-ins or a fall harvest dinner. Packs well for lunches, also.

1½ cups chopped pecans
½ cup butter, melted
2 cups sugar
2 large eggs
1 tsp. vanilla
2 cups flour
2 tsp. ground cinnamon
1 tsp. baking soda
1 tsp. salt
4 apples, peeled and cut into ¼-inch thick wedges

1 recipe Browned-Butter Frosting

- Preheat oven to 350 degrees.
- Toast pecans in a single layer in the oven for 5-7 minutes, stirring halfway through.
- In a large bowl, stir together butter, sugar, eggs and vanilla until blended.
- In a smaller bowl, combine flour, cinnamon, baking soda and salt. Add to butter mixture, stirring until blended.
- Stir in apples and 1 cup pecans. (Batter should be thick, similar to cookie dough.)
- Spread batter in a lightly greased 9 x 13 inch pan.
- Bake for 45 minutes or until wooden toothpick inserted in the center comes out clean. Cool completely in pan on wire rack.
- Spread frosting over top of cake and sprinkle with remaining ½ cup pecans.

Browned-Butter Frosting:
1 cup butter
1 16-oz. package powdered sugar
¼ cup milk
1 tsp. vanilla

- Melt butter in small, heavy saucepan over medium heat, stirring constantly. Cook for 6-8 minutes or until butter begins to turn golden brown. Remove pan from heat immediately and pour butter into small bowl. Cover and chill 1 hour or until butter is cool and begins to solidify.
- Beat cooled butter at medium speed with an electric mixer until fluffy, gradually adding powdered sugar, alternating with milk, starting and ending with powdered sugar and the vanilla.

Grandma's Old-Fashioned Cherry Pie

I spent a lot of years growing up on my grandparent's farm in western Pennsylvania. They had a very mature Stark Bro's sweet cherry tree and we enjoyed many pies, jams and cobblers from that tree. Grandma would can the cherries and when it was deep in snow outside, we could still taste the summer in those delicious cherries. A good tree for cherries to bake and cook with is the **Starking® Hardy Giant Antique**.

Pastry crust for 1 pie (see page 145)
3 cups fresh sweet cherries, pitted, OR canned cherries in natural juice (not cherry pie filling)
1 tsp. almond extract
¾ cup sugar
¼ tsp. salt
¾ cup cherry juice (may use juice from canned cherries)
2 TBS. cornstarch
1 egg, beaten with a few drops of water
1 TBS. sugar

- Preheat oven to 425 degrees.
- Line a 9-inch pie pan with the pastry crust.
- Mix the cornstarch and the juice until well blended.
- Add the sugar and salt, and simmer over low heat until thickened and clear.
- Add the almond flavoring and cherries, and stir gently. Cool.
- Pour into the pastry shell.
- Make a wide lattice top with the remaining pastry dough.
- Brush the lattice with beaten egg that has a few drops of water added.
- Sprinkle lightly with sugar.
- Bake for 10 to 12 minutes at 425 degrees, then reduce the temperature to 325 degrees. Continue baking for 35 to 40 minutes until the top is golden and the cherries bubble between the lattice.

Mrs. Miller's Apple-Raisin Pie

The First Place winner in the Dessert category, this delicious recipe was submitted by Mr. Graham Murdock of Springfield, Illinois. The associates at the Stark Bro's Garden Center in Louisiana, Missouri tended to agree with the selection when presented with the pie from the photo shoot.

Pastry for a two-crust pie (see page 145)
1 cup sugar
4 rounded TBS. flour
⅛ tsp. salt
¼ tsp. nutmeg
½ tsp. cinnamon
⅛ tsp. ground cloves
7 apples, peeled and cut into slices
⅓ cup raisins (I prefer golden raisins)
1½ TBS. fresh orange juice
1 TBS. pure maple syrup
1 tsp. molasses
2 TBS. butter, softened

Glaze:
1 cup confectioners' sugar
2½ TBS. fresh squeezed orange juice
1 rounded tsp. fresh grated orange peel

- Preheat oven to 400 degrees.
- Prepare the pastry dough.
- Line a 9-inch pie pan with 1 rolled crust and refrigerate.
- In a large bowl, combine the sugar, flour, salt, nutmeg and cinnamon. Blend well.
- Mix in the apples, raisins, maple syrup and molasses.
- Turn mixture into the pie crust. Spread evenly, creating a slight mound in the center.
- Dot with the butter and sprinkle with the orange juice.
- Top with second rolled crust and crimp the edges together, folding the bottom crust over the edge of the top crust as you crimp. Use either aluminum foil or a pie-crust ring to cover the edges and prevent over-browning.
- While pie is baking, make the glaze by blending all glaze ingredients in a small bowl.
- Bake the pie 40 to 45 minutes, removing the foil or ring about 5 minutes before pie is finished baking.
- Remove from oven onto a wire rack. Cool for 5 minutes then spread the glaze evenly over the top of the pie.

Nectarine Sorbet

Sorbets can be made with almost any fruit, but this nectarine sorbet is so refreshing and delicious you will want to make it as long as your harvest permits. Adding a few fresh mint leaves adds another enhancement to the fruit. Do not hesitate to substitute peaches, pears, strawberries, raspberries, blueberries or honeyberries.

5 cups nectarine slices
2 cups superfine sugar
1 cup orange juice or apricot nectar
3 TBS. fresh lemon juice
5-6 fresh mint leaves, lightly chopped (optional)

- In a food processor, purée the nectarines until smooth.
- In a nonreactive saucepan, place the juice, sugar and mint leaves (if using).
- Bring to simmer and stir to make sure the sugar is completely dissolved.
- Stir in the nectarine purée and blend well.
- Pour the mixture into a large rectangular pan and freeze for 4 hours.
- Process the mixture in 3 batches. Place ⅓ of the frozen mixture in the food processor and process until light and airy. (Keep remaining sorbet in the freezer while you are processing a batch.)
- Put the mixture into plastic containers and place in freezer until ready to use.

Note: Have an ice cream or sorbet machine? Use the same recipe and follow manufacturer's directions.

Pennsylvania Blackberry Cobbler

Blackberries make a delicious cobbler and hold their shape during baking. This recipe is just a good old-fashioned recipe from my home state of Pennsylvania, probably with Amish roots or Dutch origin. Plant the **Prime –Ark Freedom** or the **Prime-Ark 45** for thornless canes and use the **Stark® Blackberry and Bramble Fertilizer**. Of course, this recipe can be used with raspberries, blueberries or even sliced peaches.

3 cups fresh blackberries
1 cup sugar
1 cup flour
2 tsp. baking powder
½ tsp. baking soda
½ tsp. salt
1 cup milk
1 stick unsalted butter, melted

- Preheat oven to 375 degrees.
- Place the berries in a bowl, add the sugar and gently blend, taking care not to mash the berries. Set aside.
- Sift together the flour, baking powder, baking soda and salt in a large mixing bowl.
- Stir in the milk and the melted butter and mix, just until moistened.
- Spread the batter in a 9-inch x 12-inch baking dish.
- Top evenly with the berries.
- Bake in the preheated oven for 45-60 minutes..
- Remove from the oven and allow to sit for at least 15 minutes before serving.
- Serve with half-and-half or whipped cream or vanilla ice cream.
- Can be made a day ahead and stored, covered, in the refrigerator. Place in hot oven to reheat for 10 minutes. Do not microwave, or it will become tough.

Raspberry Cheesecake Tarts

These charming individual tarts are bursting with raspberry flavor. You may use either a regular pastry shell or a graham-cracker shell. I used a Biscoff cookie by Lotus. It is a European cookie made in Belgium that is served with coffee. It is now available in US grocery stores. It has a wonderful cinnamon flavor and adds an extra dimension to the tarts. You may also use strawberries or blueberries.

Shell:
25 broken Biscoff cookies
½ cup melted butter

Filling:
2 large eggs
12 oz. cream cheese, softened (or light cream cheese)
½ cup sour cream
1 TBS. lemon zest
3 TBS. sugar
⅔ cup raspberry fruit spread (seedless)
1 cup fresh raspberries
¾ cup white chocolate chips

- Preheat the oven to 375 degrees.
- Place cookies in a food processor and pulse into crumbs.
- With the blade running, slowly drizzle in the melted butter. Process for 60 seconds.
- Spray 6-inch tart pans with shortening spray.
- Press the crumb mixture into the bottoms only, dividing evenly between 6 tart pans.
- Bake for 8-10 minutes. Do not brown. Leave the oven on.
- With a hand mixer, blend the eggs, cream cheese and sour cream.
- Add the lemon zest and sugar, and blend again.
- Add the fruit spread and the fresh raspberries, blending just until the fruit is completely folded in.
- Divide the white chocolate chips between the 6 cooled tart shells.
- Ladle the filling into the shells until they are ¾ full.
- Bake for 25 minutes.
- Cool completely and remove from tart pans.
- Serve with whipped cream and fresh fruit to garnish.

Note: You may also use our standard sweet pastry (see page 145) OR a Graham Cracker shell.

My Favorite Rustic Fruit Pie

I first found this manner of making a pie in a small bake shop in southern France. It's quick, easy and looks very "old-fashioned." Apparently it is old fashioned, as I later discovered that early pioneers in America used this method when they were without a pie plate. You may use any fruit of choice.

1 recipe pastry crust, rolled to about 15 inches in diameter (see page 145)

4 good baking apples, peeled, cored and cut into 1-inch chunks
½ cup dried cranberries or dried goji berries
⅓ cup slivered almonds
⅔ cups brown sugar
1 tsp. ground cinnamon
½ tsp. ground nutmeg
¼ tsp. ground cloves
Pinch of salt
¼ cup sifted flour

- Preheat oven to 375 degrees.
- In a large mixing bowl, combine all ingredients together except the crust. Toss to fully coat the apples and nuts in the mixture.
- Place the rolled crust in the middle of a pizza pan or cookie sheet.
- Spoon the fruit mixture on to the center of the crust, spreading it out about 9 inches in diameter.
- Simply fold the edges of the crust up over the fruit allowing the center to be open. It does not need to be even or straight. Sprinkle a TBS. of white sugar over the top part of the crust.
- Bake for 20 minutes.
- Cover the top with foil, and bake another 20 minutes.

Makes 6 servings.

Pastry Crust

This pastry crust, referenced in numerous recipes throughout the book, is easy to make, and delicious! (The photos at left show preparation of the Rustic Fruit Pie on the previous page.)

½ cup ice water
1 egg
2½ cups all-purpose flour
¾ cup cold butter, cut into small chunks
½ cup shortening
1 tsp. salt
1½ TBS. sugar

- In a small bowl, thoroughly blend ice water and egg. Set aside.
- In a mixing bowl, cut shortening into flour with pastry cutter or two forks.
- Add salt and sugar and mix until a crumb texture forms.
- Add the egg/ice-water and mix quickly by hand. The less your hands work the mixture, the better the crust.
- Form dough into a flat ball and wrap in plastic wrap. Refrigerate at least 1 hour.
- Divide chilled dough in half, and roll out on floured board or counter. Place in the bottom of your 9-inch pie plate or tart pan.
- Roll out the second part for a top crust or cut in strips for a lattice top.
- Crimp edges together well above the rim of your pie plate, or at the edge in a tart pan if making just a single crust tart.

Makes 2 9-inch pie crusts.

Strawberries Romanoff

Back in the time of the Russian Imperial Court, the tastes of the Romanoff family leaned toward French foods. This dish was a favorite of the Court and will become a favorite of yours, also. It is simple to make and so very delicious to share with family and friends.

2 pints ripe strawberries, rinsed and hulled (reserve 8 berries with tops intact)
½ cup sugar (superfine if available), divided
⅓ cup (or more) Cointreau® or Grand Marnier®
1 orange
¾ cup heavy cream

- Place rinsed berries on a soft kitchen towel and gently pat dry.
- Place berries in a large bowl and add ⅓ cup of the sugar.
- Drizzle the liqueur over the berries.
- Remove the entire peel of the orange with a vegetable peeler, carefully avoiding the bitter white pith.
- Using a very sharp knife, slice the peel in thin long strips about ⅛-inch wide and about 1½-inch long.
- Add the thin peel to the berries and gently fold into the berries.
- Cover tightly and refrigerate for 1 hour, or until ready to serve.
- Whip the cream and add the remaining sugar.
- Serve in clear glass stemmed dishes, topping with the whipped cream and 1 reserved berry, or alternately serve as pictured on a buffet.

Serves 6 to 8.

Strawberry Sorbet with Balsamic Glaze

This quick and easy dessert is wonderful for a weeknight supper, ladies' luncheon or a special company dinner. Using a good-quality purchased sorbet makes it a very user-friendly recipe and makes you look like a culinary genius! Wild, fresh strawberries make it even better; try the farmer's market in strawberry season, or grow your own.

⅔ cup good balsamic vinegar
1 TBS. sugar
1 quart fresh strawberries, rinsed, hulled and halved (quartered if very large)
1 pint strawberry sorbet
Fresh mint leaves for garnish (optional)

- In a saucepan, boil the balsamic vinegar with the sugar for 4 to 5 minutes, until the vinegar is reduced by half and is slightly syrupy. Do not overcook or it will become like glue! Cool the glaze.
- Spoon the sorbet into dessert dishes or stemmed glasses.
- Divide the berries amongst the dishes.
- Drizzle with the cooled glaze and top with optional mint leaves.

Serves 6.

Strawberry Shortcake

This traditional shortcake can be used with an assortment of fruits, but us oldies remember this as how Grandma made it. Mother used to make individual shortcakes, and we always poured some milk on them in addition to the whipped cream. In any case, it makes a beautiful presentation and the taste is wonderful. Try this same recipe with a mixture of blueberries and sliced fresh peaches.

1½ quarts fresh strawberries, rinsed, hulled and sliced
6 TBS. sugar (divided)
1½ cups flour
1 TBS. baking powder
1 tsp. baking soda
½ tsp. salt
¼ cup cold butter, cut into small chunks
1 large egg
½ cup whole milk
Whipped cream

- Preheat the oven to 425 degrees.
- Combine 4 TBS. of the sugar with the flour, baking powder, baking soda and salt.
- Cut in the butter until the mixture resembles pea-sized pieces.
- In a small bowl, combine the egg and milk.
- Add the milk mixture to the dry ingredients and fold in quickly. Mix until just combined.
- Drop by spoonfuls onto lightly-greased baking parchment, creating 8 nice shortbreads.
- Bake for about 12 minutes, until lightly golden and just turning light brown at the bottom edges. Cool.
- Sprinkle the remaining 2 TBS. sugar over the strawberries to create some "syrup." Mix gently and allow to sit at room temperature for 10 minutes.
- Cut each shortcake in half horizontally, placing the bottom on an individual plate. Spoon strawberries on shortcake, then place the top half and spoon some more strawberries on top. Drizzle a bit of the strawberry syrup over top and add whipped cream.

Serves 8.

Tiramisu with Strawberries

During my spring stay in France, I found this recipe in a local magazine. I tried it and loved it! The original recipe called for using raw egg yolks, which I don't recommend, so they have been omitted here. You could substitute raspberries, blueberries or thinly-sliced fresh sweet peaches for the strawberries.

2 cups fresh strawberries, rinsed, hulled and sliced (reserve 8 whole berries for garnish)
½ cup heavy cream
2 tsp. superfine sugar
1 cup mascarpone cheese, softened
1 cup crushed Amaretti cookies
¼ cup orange juice or orange liqueur
1 TBS. unsweetened cocoa

- Whip the cream until soft peaks form, then add the sugar.
- Fold the sweetened whipped cream into the softened mascarpone.
- Place ¼ of the crumbled cookies in the bottom of four clear glasses, reserving 4 TBS. crumbs.
- Drizzle ¼ of the liqueur or juice in each glass.
- Place 3 or 4 slices of strawberries on the crumbs.
- Spoon some of the mascarpone mixture into each glass.
- Repeat with strawberries and the mascarpone mixture.
- Sprinkle the top of each glass with the crumbs mixed together with the cocoa.
- Garnish with reserved strawberries or whatever fruit was used.

Serves 4

Canning & Preserving

My Grandma's Christmas Jam

How to Can and Preserve

You've planted the trees and the bushes and taken care of them — pruning, fertilizing and weeding for a number of years. Now this work is "bearing fruit" and you cannot eat it all at once. So you turn to canning, freezing and drying your bountiful harvest. Just how is that all done?

Taking the time to learn the proper way to preserve your fruits is vital to success in any of the methods mentioned above. There is a lot of information available to the home gardener, and it's mostly free. Your Agricultural Extension office is a great source of information and guidance. The Internet offers thousands of ideas and recipes. Ball® (the canning jar company) has a wonderful book called "Blue Book Guide to Preserving" and the Mother Earth News Wiser Living Series offers a magazine called *How to Grow and Preserve Your Own Food.* These are just a few sources for good information to assist you in saving the harvest for future meals. Once you do your homework, you will soon become a pro at preserving and your family will enjoy the "fruits" of your labor all year-'round. Above all, it is very important you learn the safe and proper way to preserve.

When canning, you will want to know when to use the boiling-water method or the pressure method. High-acid foods need the boiling-water method and low-acid foods require the pressure method. This will require a small investment in some equipment, but it will serve you well for many years. Your Stark Bro's catalog offers canning supplies as well as racks and canning pots. This should get you started, and then you can begin to enjoy the satisfaction of raising and preserving your very own fruits. Check out Stark Bro's easy-to-follow *Put 'em Up! Preserving Answer Book* for more information.

Drying your harvest offers you lots of opportunities for creativity. Some of the recipes in this book use dried fruit, so give it a try. Dehydrated fruit is bursting with flavor if you research the right way to do it. There are a number of dehydrators on the market, not to mention solar energy, which happens to be free! And once you learn to dry your fruit, you can move onto your veggies and herbs. It is a centuries-old process that assures you delicious, concentrated flavors all year long.

Canning supplies, including those at right, are available in our catalog and on our website.

STARK
A GROWING LEGACY SINCE 1816
SIMPLY DELICIOUS

Brandied Peaches

A delicious topping for ice cream, pound cake or served alongside roast beef or pork roast. Served as a dessert in a pool of crème anglaise, it is stunning. The **Stark® Hal-Berta Giant™** or **Sentry** peaches work well in this recipe, but you may use any peach that is firm and sweet. Also the **Stark® Saturn** is a fun peach shape to use in this recipe. Makes a wonderful gift at the holidays.

10–12 ripe but firm peaches, peeled, pitted and halved from stem end to blossom end
2 cups sugar
2 cups water
½ cup brandy, + or –

4 wide-mouth pint canning jars, lids and rings, sterilized

- Place the sugar and water in a nonreactive kettle.
- Bring to a boil and simmer the peaches in this simple syrup for about 5 to 8 minutes. Do not overcook.
- Place the peach halves in sterile jars and add the poaching syrup to each jar, leaving about 1 inch of headspace. Spoon about 4 TBS. brandy into each jar.
- Wipe the rim and seal. Place in a water bath and process for 15 minutes.
- Store in a cool, dark cupboard for 2 to 3 months to infuse the brandy into the peaches.

Makes approximately 4 pints.

F. R. O. G. Jam
(Figs, Raspberries, Orange, Ginger)

My friend Peggy Meyer spent an afternoon with me in my kitchen a few years ago. We made F. R. O. G. Jam and Gram's Christmas Jam. Peggy supplied the raspberries from her farm, and a friend brought the figs back from a trip south. It is by far one of the best jams I have ever eaten and, while it makes wonderful gifts for the holidays, it is hard to give away!

5 cups dried figs or fresh chopped figs, stems removed, quartered
2 cups orange juice
10 oz. fresh or frozen raspberries (about 1½ cups)
1 TBS. grated fresh ginger
1 cup sugar

6 half-pint canning jars, lids and rings, sterilized

- In a large stainless steel pot, add the figs and orange juice. Bring to a boil, then reduce heat to a simmer and cover. Cook until the skins of the figs are soft and the seeds have been released, approximately 15 minutes. Stir frequently to avoid scorching the pan bottom.
- Using a stick blender, purée the figs (or allow to cool and put in a blender and purée, and return to the pan).
- Add the raspberries and ginger. Increase the heat to medium and stir frequently. Cook until the raspberries have fallen apart.
- Add the sugar to personal taste.
- Pour into sterilized jelly jars and seal with lids and rings.
- Place jars in a boiling-water bath and process for 15 minutes.
- Remove and allow to cool and seal. Check tops by pressing on the center of each lid to be sure they do not click. If the lid clicks, it did not seal. Store these jars in refrigerator and use in 30 days.

Makes 5 or 6 8-oz. jars.

Gram's Christmas Jam

At our house we call this "Christmas Jam" because my grandmother only made it at Christmastime for family and friends. It reminds me of a stained-glass window with the red cherries shining through the golden orange apricots. Use your own dried apricots or buy them at the store.

32 oz. dried apricots
1 14-oz. jar maraschino cherries, drained
2 14-oz. cans crushed pineapple, well-drained
3 cups sugar
1 pkg. Sure-Jell fruit pectin

10 half-pint canning jars (or 5 pint jars), lids and rings, sterilized

- Cook the apricots in a small amount of water until soft, 10 minutes.
- Cut each cherry into thirds and set aside.
- Drain apricots and place in food processor fitted with the steel blade.
- Pulse on and off for 1-2 minutes, until chopped but not puréed.
- Return to pan, and add the pineapple and sugar.
- Simmer in a slow bubble until it begins to thicken, about 10 minutes, stirring constantly.
- Add the Sure-Jell and bring back to bubbly for 1 minute.
- Add the cherries and cook the mixture for 1 minute.
- Put into sterile, hot jars, seal immediately and put into a water bath for 10 min (see Canning page 156).

Makes about 5 pints.

Note: I use small jelly jars, tie raffia or ribbon around the top and add a cherry holiday label on the front. I put them in a holiday gift bag with a package of English muffins and an individual package of flavored coffee, and hand them out on Christmas Eve as guests depart from our annual Christmas buffet. Instant breakfast!

Spiced Pear Butter

This wonderful alternative to apple butter will delight your palate all year long. Served on warm English muffins or with toasted French bread or on a peanut butter sandwich, it is delicious. It can be brushed on a pork roast at the end of roasting to pop the flavor, or alongside cheese-and-sausage appetizer platters. The **Starking® Delicious** is the perfect pear for this recipe.

¾ cup water
3 lbs. fresh pears, unpeeled, cored and quartered
4 TBS. light brown sugar
3 TBS. honey
1 tsp. lemon juice
1 tsp. ground cinnamon
1 tsp. ground ginger
1 tsp. ground allspice
½ tsp. ground cloves
¼ tsp. salt

4 wide-mouth canning pints, lids and rings, sterilized

- Place all the ingredients in a heavy-bottomed nonreactive kettle and cover.
- Over medium-low heat, simmer the ingredients for 30 minutes, stirring occasionally.
- When the pears soften completely, remove from heat and cool 15 minutes.
- Place pear mixture in a food processor and process until it becomes a very smooth purée.
- Place back into the kettle and simmer on low heat, uncovered, for 1 hour or until thickened. Stir frequently.
- Ladle into sterilized pint jars, wipe rims and seal with lids and rings. Place in a boiling-water bath canner and process for 20 minutes.
- Remove and sit on counter to cool and seal. Store in a cool, dark cupboard for 6 months.

Makes approximately 4 pints.

Spiced Pears

A whole spiced pear makes an elegant dessert and can be further enhanced with a strawberry coulis or drizzled with a dark chocolate sauce. **Blake's Pride** is a wonderful, buttery-flavored pear for this dish, or you could use **Seckel** pears. Whichever pear you select, it must be firm and in some cases a bit underripe. Leave the stem on the pear for presentation.

10 to 12 small whole pears, peeled, stem on
3 cups boiling water
3 cups sugar
3 cinnamon sticks
1 TBS. crystallized ginger (1 disc) or a 1-inch piece of peeled fresh ginger
8 whole cloves
⅓ cup cider vinegar
4 wide-mouth canning pints (or 2 quart jars), lids and rings, sterilized

- In a small saucepan, combine the water and sugar. Bring to a boil and dissolve the sugar completely. Add the spices and vinegar.
- In a large nonreactive kettle, place the peeled pears, standing up. Pour the sugar syrup mixture over the pears.
- Bring to a boil, then reduce heat to low. Cover and simmer for 45 minutes until the pears are slightly softened, but not mushy.
- Using a strainer spoon, gently place the pears in sterile jars. Remove the spices from the liquid and pour the poaching liquid into the jars, leaving ½-inch headspace. Wipe the rims and seal. Process in a boiling-water bath for 15 minutes.

Depending on the size of your pears, you should realize 4 pints, or 2 quarts.

Simple Blueberry Jam

Capture the essence of in-season blueberries with this simple, no-fail jam.

6 cups fresh blueberries, rinsed, stemmed and picked through
⅔ cup sugar
1 TBS. lemon juice
1 tsp. lemon zest
¼ tsp. salt

4 half-pint canning jars, with lids and tops, sterilized

- Place all ingredients in a large, heavy-bottomed saucepan.
- Mash up the berries with a potato masher to release the juices.
- Bring to a simmer and cook over medium heat, stirring constantly to avoid scorching.
- Cook for 20 minutes. At the very end of the cooking time, bring to a slow rolling boil.
- Spoon into sterilized jam jars and seal with lids and rings.
- Holds in refrigerator for 4 to 6 weeks.

Makes about 4 cups.

Summer Peach & Orange Jam

The tartness of the orange zest and the sweetness of the sun-ripened peaches will transport you back to summer when the snow is blowing and the temperatures dip to the low teens. It also makes a great hostess gift during the holidays, or any occasion that calls for something from your kitchen.

1 large lemon
3 large, juicy oranges
12 to 14 firm, ripe, peaches, peeled, pitted and cut into ½-inch chunks
6 cups sugar

6 half-pint canning jars, with lids and tops, sterilized

- Using a citrus zester, remove the zest from both the lemon and the oranges.
- Squeeze the juice from both citrus and remove any seeds, but not the pulp.
- Place the juices and the zest in a large heavy-bottomed kettle.
- Add peaches to the juices and zest.
- Stir in the sugar and bring to boil over medium heat, stirring frequently to avoid scorching.
- After 5 minutes of boiling, reduce the heat to a low simmer for 30-40 minutes, stirring.
- Pour into hot sterilized jars, leaving about ½-inch headspace. Wipe the jar rims and put on lids and rings.
- Place the jars into a boiling-water canner and process for 15 minutes.
- Check for sealed lids by pressing down on lid top. If it clicks, it is not sealed properly and must be reprocessed or refrigerated (keeps up to 1 month).
- Store in a cool, dark cupboard.

Make 5 – 6 cups.

About Karen Mitcham-Stoeckley

Karen has been a restaurant owner, executive chef and culinary writer for most of her adult career, devoting herself to creating good food to feed family and friends, as well as professionally feeding guests who demand only the best on their plate. Cooking, teaching and writing are her passions.

Her former restaurant in Louisiana, Missouri was located in the historic downtown area just blocks from the Mississippi River. The property housed a bistro, fine-dining restaurant, a dining garden, winery and bakery, along with an 11-room B&B inn. Good food, good service and award-winning wine was the keystone of the business. Today, Karen still operates the bakery, winery and B&B inn, along with a very experienced staff. In the spring months, Karen teaches week-long Provençal cooking classes in southern France to couples from the USA. Karen may be contacted about her classes at: livininprovence@yahoo.com.

Her previous culinary experience includes a number of years in the 1970s as the Culinary Consultant to Le Creuset and Cousances, the wonderfully heavy vitreous enameled cast-iron French cookware. That position afforded her the opportunity to teach cooking from Bloomingdale's Main Course in New York City to Macy's basement in San Francisco, as well as to study cooking in France, Italy and the USA.

A summer spent with Maurice Moore-Betty in his NYC school was another opportunity that molded her culinary abilities. A brief stint in New Orleans gave Karen a peek into Cajun cooking, and three years living in East Asia allowed her to study Japanese, Thai and Chinese cuisine.

Karen and her husband, artist John Stoeckley, have traveled to Provence for 19 springs/summers. There, Karen has enjoyed the opportunity to cook and teach in her own kitchen with the abundance of produce from the local marketplace, as well as to visit and work in the kitchens of many successful chefs.

In 2012-2013, Karen spent seven months in Les Arcs sur Argens, France, creating her first major cookbook, *A Culinary Legacy ... from Escoffier to Today*, which was also photographed by Curt Dennison on location.

About Curt Dennison

Curt Dennison began his career in art the moment that he was dismissed from kindergarten for coloring outside of the lines. Following that theme, he declined to finish high school and opted instead for university, graduating in 1982 from Southern Illinois University at Edwardsville with a Bachelor of Fine Arts, majoring in painting and printmaking. While in school, he became intimate with the art and craft of photography, which became a career choice.

Photographing food is his greatest love, having worked for Pet Incorporated as their corporate photographer from 1987 to 1994. Curt has created photographs professionally since 1982 and has owned a freelance commercial photography business since 1994. He photographs people, products, places, food and agriculture for agency, corporate, advertising and industrial clients worldwide. A portfolio of work can be viewed at curtdennisonphotography.com.

He lives in Washington, Missouri USA with his loving wife Wendy, and is a member and Past President of the Rotary Club of Washington. He has five children and two grandchildren.

Curt would like to thank the following people for their great help in creating this book: His good friend and fabulous chef Karen Mitcham-Stoeckley, Wendy Dennison, Doug Sikes and Frene Melton at Acclaim Press, and, of course, his mother, Sallie Owen Newman Dennison.

Index

Acknowledgments

Creating and writing a cookbook takes the assistance and trust of many people. As author, I would like to thank the following folks for being a part of making this book a reality.

Many thanks to my friend, Evan Scherder, for chopping, dicing and doing all those dishes during photography sessions.

A big thanks to all my friends who showed up to taste test the photo food; you know who you are.

Thanks to my little sister, Susan, who shared some of her fruit recipes with me and pointed me in the right direction regarding canning and preserving techniques.

To Ken Lane and Cameron Brown at Stark Bros. I am deeply appreciative of your faith and trust in me to create this book to celebrate the 200th anniversary of your company.

To my husband, John, who spent months stepping over photo equipment and props and who ate many unbalanced meals of photo food, thank you for your patience and support.

And most of all to my partner in fun, Curt Dennison, the finest photographer in the world, who makes all my creations look great, I extend a most heartfelt thank you for all your hard work in photographing and designing the entire book.

Karen Mitcham-Stoeckley

STARK Bro's

A GROWING LEGACY SINCE 1816

Stark Bro's Nurseries & Orchards Co.
Website: StarkBros.com
Email: info@StarkBros.com
Phone: 800.325.4180
Fax: 573.754.3701
Mail: PO BOX 1800, Louisiana, MO 63353